N A N
The Life of
an Irish Travelling
Woman

N a n

The Life of
an Irish Travelling
Woman

SHARON GMELCH

W · W · Norton & Company

NEW YORK   LONDON

Published simultaneously in Canada by Penguin Books
Canada Ltd., 2801 John Street, Markham, Ontario L3R 1B4

Printed in the United States of America.

Designed by Margaret M. Wagner
The text of this book is composed in ITC Garamond
Light, with display type set in Garamond #3.
Composition and manufacturing by the Maple-Vail Book
Manufacturing Group.

First Edition

Library of Congress Cataloging-in-Publication Data

Gmelch, Sharon.
Nan : The Life of an Irish Travelling Woman.

Bibliography: p.
1. Donohoe, Nan. 2. Ireland—Anthropology.
3. Tinkers—Ireland—Anthropology. 1. Title.
CT868.D68G54 1986   305.5′62   [B]   85–31986

ISBN 0-393-02331-1

W. W. Norton & Company, Inc.,
500 Fifth Avenue,
New York, N. Y. 10110
W. W. Norton & Company Ltd.,
37 Great Russell Street,
London WC1B 3NU

1 2 3 4 5 6 7 8 9 0

TO SAM, JOHN,
MICHAEL, KEVIN, KATHLEEN,
SALLY, BRENDAN, JAMES,
EDDIE, AND WILLIE,
IN LOVING MEMORY OF
THEIR MOTHER.

CONTENTS

ACKNOWLEDGMENTS

Many people have helped me. Michael, Sam, John, Brendan, Kevin, Sally, Kathleen, and Eddie Donoghue (Donohoe) took an interest in my recording of their mother's story and were often present as we talked, providing encouragement and a constant supply of tea. Many people in government agencies, institutions, libraries, and towns and villages in both Ireland and England helped me ferret out further information on Nan. Although I cannot thank them all by name, I am very grateful. Victor Bewley, who has worked so tirelessly to aid Travelling People, assisted me in my early research among them. Social workers Patricia McCarthy and Eithne Russell helped me on numerous occasions as they did Nan. My good friends Vincent and Margaret Jones always made my stays in Ireland pleasant.

Cynthia Carbone, Brian Cullen, George Gmelch, Tom Furey, Tom and Josephine Murphy, Michael O'Brien, Shiela Otto, Ruth Pasquariello, and Warren Roberts read the first chapter I wrote and had many useful comments. Tom Furey and Tom Murphy, both knowledgeable in Irish history, were particularly helpful, as was the enthusiasm of my friends Cynthia Carbone and Shiela Otto, who saw in Nan's childhood the greatness of her story. Michael O'Brien encouraged me to go ahead with work on Nan's biography rather than stick to more conventional academic writing. Richard Nelson, my good friend and fellow anthropologist, gave the entire manuscript a thorough reading and encouraged me in my attempt to write both good anthropology and literature. Tom Weakley's invaluable criticism of each chapter helped me clarify my goals and find my voice. He reminded me over and over to "tell a story."

I also wish to thank Wayne Hunte, director of McGill University's Bellairs Research Institute in Barbados, for providing me with working space and a pleasant environment during an important phase of my writing. Mary Cunnane, my editor at W. W. Norton, recognized the universality of Nan's story, for which I am very grateful. And lastly, but certainly not least, I would like to thank my husband, George, for his valuable emotional support throughout the years of work and my son, Morgan, for sharpening my insights.

PREFACE

NAN DONOHOE was an Irish Travelling woman and to fully appreciate her story some background information is in order. The Travelling People, long known as "tinkers," have for generations stood on the bottom rung of Ireland's social and economic ladder—a poor and stigmatized minority group. Until recently, they traveled through the countryside, at first on foot and later in horse-drawn carts and wagons, performing a variety of trades and services. Although their lifestyle was and continues to be outwardly similar to that of the Romany Gypsy, Travellers are native to Ireland. They are one of numerous indigenous itinerant groups—including the Swedish Resande, Norwegian Taters, Dutch Woonwagenbewoners, and Scottish Travellers—to have evolved in Western Europe. Today, they remain one of the least assimilated.

Unfortunately, the early history of Ireland's Travelling People is obscure. Being illiterate, they left no written records of their own. Being poor, they largely have been ignored in the literature of the "Great Tradition." Only one thing is certain, not all families originated at the same time nor in the same way. Some Travelling families date back centuries, others have adopted an itinerant life-style in modern times. Some undoubtedly began as itinerant craftsmen and specialists who traveled because of the limited demand for their work in any one place. Others were originally peasants and laborers who voluntarily went on the road to look for work or else were forced onto it by eviction or some personal reason—a problem with drink, the birth of an illegitimate child, marriage to a "tinker."

Tinsmiths have formed a distinct group for many centuries; "tinker" and "tynkere" first appear as trade- or surnames in written records during the twelfth century. But as early as the fifth century, itinerant whitesmiths—as well as other craftsmen and specialists such as tanners, musicians, and bards—travelled the Irish countryside fashioning jewelry, weapons, and horse trappings out of bronze, silver, and gold in exchange for food and lodging. Tinkers were numerous enough in Ireland (and Scotland) by the sixteenth century to have given Romany Gypsies stiff competition when they arrived in the British Isles for the first time. By 1835, when Britain's Poor Inquiry Commissioners visited Ireland to collect evidence on the state of the poor, they were told that "wives and families accompany the tinker while he strolls about in search of work, and always beg. They intermarry with one another, and form a distinct class."[1]

Today there are approximately 2,500 Travelling families living in Ireland or 16,500 Travellers in a population of 3.5 million settled Irish. Another 1,000 families live in Northern Ireland, England, and Wales.[2]

Prior to World War II, Travellers were rural people who traveled from one farm and village to the next making and repairing tinware, cleaning chimneys, dealing in donkeys and horses, selling small household wares, and picking crops in exchange for food, clothing, and cash. They also made clothespins, brushes, brooms, and baskets; repaired umbrellas; collected horse hair, feathers, bottles, used clothes, and rags; and exploited the sentiments and fears of the settled population through begging, fortune telling, and bogus money-making schemes. As one of Nan's sons once succinctly explained,

The tinker was a man who thought of a hundred ways of surviv-
ing. If he was selling delph [crockery] and the delph failed him,
he'd switch to somethin' else. Maybe he'd buy somethin' else or
resell it. There were always a hundred ways out. This was the
real tinker, not the tinsmith. He was a better survivor than the
rest.

Travellers camped on the roadside in dispersed groups of
one to three families from mid-March until November, when
most moved back to their home village or took shelter in
abandoned houses in the countryside. When traveling they
seldom remained in a camp for longer than two weeks and
sometimes for only a day or two. For although Travellers were
welcomed for the useful services they performed and the news
and stories they carried, once their work was done they were
encouraged to go. The police frequently evicted them.

With the introduction of plastics and cheap mass-produced
tin and enamelware following World War II, the tinsmith's
work was eliminated. Other rural-based trades also became
obsolete. Tractors and farm machinery, such as the beet digger, replaced the need for horses and most agricultural workers; private cars and an expanded rural bus service, which
made shopping in town easier, did away with the rural peddler. As a result, most families migrated to the cities. There,
the men began collecting scrap metal, and the women begged.
Today most families earn their livelihood from scrap metal
collecting, the salvaging and sale of car parts, trading household wares from door to door, and government welfare. Half
still live on the roadside, but in modern trailers. The remainder have moved on to official government campsites and some
have been housed.

Despite frequent economic dealings between Travellers and
settled people, social relations between the two have always
been strained. The petty pilfering, trickery, and property
damage caused by some Travellers and their trespassing horses

never endeared them to the settled community. And as land-less nomads just passing through, they were always suspect. On occasion, however, distant but affectionate bonds developed between individual Travellers and settled people. Those who moved within small circuits of one or two counties and visited the same communities and farms several times a year often earned local reputations as memorable and entertaining characters, acquiring nicknames like "Bawling Moll" or "Tom the pipe." Today many Travelling women have developed patroness–client relationships with settled women they regularly visit.[3] But even here, social distance is carefully maintained by the settled Irish and, to a lesser extent, by the Travellers themselves.

Although some intermarriage has occured, Travellers and settled people generally do not marry. Genetic studies demonstrate that Travellers are more closely related to the Irish than to any other population, including Romany Gypsies, but they have formed a sufficiently isolated breeding population to have diverged from the settled community at several gene loci.[4] As a result of the physical and social distance that separates them, most Irish know very little about Travellers. The Travellers' argot or cant, known as Gammon, is unknown to most.[5] Settled people have also imputed exotic customs and behavior to Travellers. Country people, for example, once believed that Travellers married by jumping over a tinker's budget [tool bag] or by holding hands over the back of a donkey while a tinker "king" made the sign of the cross. Even today, supernatural powers are sometimes attributed to them. Travellers, on the other hand, are keen observers of settled life; their very existence depends on knowing the host society, both its foibles and strengths.

When measured against modern standards of living in Ireland, Travellers are a deprived minority despite the considerable government and volunteer effort since the mid-1960s to improve their lot.[6] Most families lack running water, electricity, sanitation, and refuse collection and live in terribly crowded conditions. During the winter, life is particularly harsh. Infant mortality and respiratory diseases, particularly bronchitis and pneumonia, have always been high. Traveller babies have a lower average birth weight than infants in the settled population. Adults still suffer a far higher rate of accidental death than settled people and have shorter life spans. Most adults are also illiterate or at best, semiliterate. And although a major effort has been made to see that Traveller children go to school, only half are enrolled. Furthermore, many attend sporadically and most drop out before age twelve.

The picture that emerges from this brief description is in some ways difficult to understand. Irish Travellers are fundamentally similar to other members of Irish society; they are white, English-speaking, Roman Catholic, and native to Ireland. The most common family names—McDonagh, Connor, Ward, O'Brien, Maugham, and Donohoe—are as Irish as any. They are poor and powerless and therefore constitute no economic or political threat. Yet they are pariahs.[7]

After World War II, Travellers—along with the rest of Ireland—were hurled into the twentieth century, ill-prepared for its urban life and myriad social problems. They adopted new trades and adapted to new patterns of mobility and social life.[8] Many prospered, but many were pulled into dependency and despair. Two decades of help from volunteer groups and government agencies has created official campsites, placed some families in houses, and improved educational opportunities, but relations between Travellers and settled people have only worsened. Conspicuously crowded into cities, Travellers are more visible than ever, their roadside camps littered with car bodies and piles of scrap metal and domestic debris. Seeing this and responding to deep-seated fears, no neighborhood wants an official campsite built nearby. Anti-Traveller protests have been frequent and ugly. As a result, large numbers of Travellers remain on the roadside and the gap between Travellers and settled people has widened. Travellers are no longer seen to have their legitimate place.

Fortunately, a growing solidarity and activism among Travellers is emerging, particularly among those living in Dublin. In 1980 a Travelling family sued the city and won a Supreme Court decision laying down the principle that families be given an alternative place to camp before they are evicted. A *Charter of Traveller Human Rights* has been presented to the government. A niece of Nan's ran for public office; her son Michael belongs to *Minceir Misli,* a Traveller political action group. Travellers have begun to take fate into their own hands. But the road ahead is rough. As Nan's story shows, it always has been.

While no individual can fully represent an entire culture, Nan's life is not atypical. Most of what happened to Nan—the many births and marital disputes, the alternating periods of travel and settlement, her emigration to England and experiences with settled people—is typical of Travellers. Nan's training as a kitchen maid, however, is exceptional. Nan also travelled more widely than many and she endured more physical hardship and abuse than most Travelling women. Having said this, I believe that most Travellers—especially women of Nan's age—will easily see their own lives reflected in Nan's story. Younger Travellers may glimpse something of their recent history.

Nan gave her life story to me freely and in the knowledge that I intended to publish it. We discussed using a pseudonym, but Nan decided to use her own name and indeed, looked forward to seeing her book. I deeply regret that she was not able to do so.

Foreword

Sharon Gmelch has devoted much time and study, and exact and intimate observation, to the past history and the present lot of the Travelling People of Ireland. She has done more. She has given the Travellers the attention of the heart and a genuine, unsentimental consideration. Not just scientific curiosity inspired this book but a true feeling for Travelling People in the houseless woods and for a way of life that has vanished, or changed dramatically, in my own lifetime.

Indeed, Nan Donohue, Sharon's friend, was born in the same year as myself and her path in life (a hard path and a sad life, yet, as this book shows, not without its own happiness and humor and beauty), her path in life, I say, must at some time or other have crossed the path of Margaret Barry, the singing woman of the Travelling People of our own time. For Margaret once told me how Alan Lomax, that relentless collector of old songs, came on her when she was singing at a fair in the town of Dundalk, singing "The Mantle So Green," and could be heard, she said, from one end of Dundalk to the other, and Lomax brought her with him all the way to London and the Albert Hall. A long road for any traveler.

Nan came into the world in the rich green Irish midlands, born under a bush close to the town of Granard and not far from another town sacred to the name of Maria Edgeworth, Edgeworthstown, now semi-Gaelicized to Mostrim when anybody remembers so to call it. That town was home and winter lodgings, and a roof over the head, for Nan's people. For she was born into a partially settled way of life: her father, John Donohue, her mother, Sarah Power, a grandmother, Oney Ward, all honorable names among the Travellers.

The father had served his time in the British army and brought out of it a pretty strict sense of discipline, maintained mostly by the army bell and the peak of his cap. Oddly enough, the peak of the cloth cap could prove an effective weapon in a Rough House, and it was a jocose boast in the Ulster of my boyhood for a man to say: "I could beat a streetful of ye with me cap." The father also had his trade as a chimney sweep and when the spring came, and the stones in the streams turned over for the feast of St. Patrick, the family could quietly, almost secretively, quit Edgeworthstown and take to the roads. For after the fires of the winter the chimneys of the country needed cleaning, and the farmers, too, had other jobs to be done, and Meath and Westmeath and Longford were rich counties.

We are reminded of the poet, Blind Rafferty, proclaiming that now with the coming in of spring the days will stretch a bit and that after the feast of Brigid he would hoist the sail and go. Or of the cattledrover in Padraic Colum's poem herding another man's beasts eastward and dreaming, out of the old folktales, of white ships and the King of Spain's daughter. Few men that I have known could speak so well or so wisely of the shivilers (tramps) and Travelling People as Padraic Colum. His father had, after all, been master of Longford's poorhouse. A lot of Travellers passed that way.

Nan's father and family were, in fact, part of an ordered society. God's poor, in most places and to many people, were still God's poor. In later years she lived in a confining and ill-fitted house in a Dublin suburb (which Sharon Gmelch describes so exactly that the reading is painful to anyone who has witnessed what has happened to some of the fringes of Dublin). Earlier, Nan rebukes her daughter, Mary, who has thoughtlessly left her standing outside on the doorstep of a hotel kitchen where Mary worked. The words come out of a lost world:

Our Lord travelled before we ever travelled and he wasn't ashamed of his mother. I never wanted to be on the road; I never asked to be on it. Whatever was before me in life I got. And now it's up to you to make the best of your life. And I hope you will never be on the road.

But out of those almost halcyon early days comes the story of the stealing of the little pig, of its replacement by the crowing bantam, doomed, because of ancient belief, to a cruel death: certainly one of the most moving stories of the innocence and pathos of childhood that I have ever heard. As the story of the encounter and duel with the fat female Scottish cook, in a fine house in a lovely English village, is the high comic point in the life of Nan. She was a very determined young woman. She needed that determination to survive, even to her early sixties, the life that was to follow.

It is not necessary for me here to follow it step by step. She tells her own story well and with a turn of phrase that would have delighted John Millington Synge. She has by no means closed her life on poetry. Her auditor and editor and friend deals delicately with the material, adds comments sparingly and most wisely on the life of Nan and, with sound knowledge of the changes over, say, the last forty years, in rural and urban ways of life that have led to the crisis and the degradation of many of the Travelling People.

There are so many things that have fascinated and moved me in this story. It is some joy for an Ulsterman, in these difficult times, to read that Nan found the North the best place in which to travel. I have heard a Kerryman say the same and he was not that sort of traveler but a scholar and antiquarian and, wait for it, a higher civil servant.

Was the gap they passed through on the way to the North the historic and mythological Gap of the North under Slieve Gullion mountains or something as flat as Duleek Common where the last shots were fired in the Battle of Boyme?

The far west in Connemara was hard and ungiving but the ground there was rock and the people poor, and the tragic stone throwing of some graceless young folk marked forever the memory of this wandering and suffering and valiant woman.

In the end of her days she looks out of a window toward Broombridge in the north of Dublin city and her whole life comes back to her: and I think of Padraic O'Conaire, Gaelic storyteller, who himself took to the homeless road and who wrote that melancholy tale about the woman at the window.

And in the generous North, Nan encounters the even more generous Yanks, young men in uniform who rob the canteen to give to the poor. In James Stephens's novel, *The Demi-Gods,* the angels of heaven descended to walk the roads with the tinkers. With a voice out of pastoral innocence, Nan says: "They were very goodhearted the Yanks. But they left. They went back." She did not know the way their traveling was leading them nor that many of those young men who were so open-handed might never again have seen the smoke rising above the rooftree of home.

Benedict Kiely

N A N
The Life of
an Irish Travelling
Woman

I

Nan

Fifteen years have passed since I first met Nan at Holy-lands—a small, nettle-choked field on the southern outskirts of Dublin. Twenty Travelling families were camped there in trailers and horse-drawn wagons on land set aside for them by the city.

It was a warm and reassuring August afternoon. I was sitting in the shade of the watchman's hut—the shack where a city employee kept ineffectual watch on the families and manned the only telephone—talking to Michael Donohoe. He was eighteen, and Elvis Presley was his idol. He needn't have told me. He was wearing pointed shoes, a metallic blue shirt with four buttons open, and tight black pants. His red hair was slicked back into a ducktail, the front uncoiling in a big curl on his forehead. He was friendly, but disappointed I didn't know Elvis personally.

Across the road from us, a stout woman dressed in a wool skirt, zip-front smock, textured nylons, and boots bent over a campfire spreading dough on an iron griddle suspended above the fire. Next to her, another woman vigorously swept the pavement around a mound of broken pipes, mangled bicycle frames, and rusting engine blocks. Two little girls sat at the back of her trailer, giggling as they pulled squealing puppies out of a cardboard box. It was a peaceful scene, interrupted only by the momentary sounds of an engine and a blur of male voices as a Ford Escort van raced by.

I had been visiting Holylands and another camp for weeks, talking to whoever was willing, trying to accustom people to me and explain my interest in them. I was an American, a graduate student in anthropology, and I had come to live with Travelling People—Ireland's indigenous "gypsies." For although they had travelled the roads for centuries, no one knew much about them. They were outcasts—"tinkers"—living in poverty on the fringe of society, and I wanted to learn first-hand what their lives were like. But to them I was merely a stranger, arriving with no apparent purpose or use, other than to talk to people.

Michael had just begun to question me about Clint Eastwood, when two younger boys—his brothers—ran up. They circled us, pressing in eagerly to ask questions and stare. And when it somehow emerged that I had just gotten a kitten and had it in my car, they begged me to get it and show it to their mother. I hesitated, envisioning my kitten bounding to the ground only to be snapped up by one of the many mongrel greyhounds and lurchers that roamed the camp. But I also felt foolish at the thought of walking up to an adult, merely to show her a kitten. Still, it was an opportunity to meet another Traveller; and opportunities were not to be missed, particularly this early in my research.

As we reached the boys' trailer, a frail, elderly woman stepped down from the battered doorway. I was startled. I had pictured a younger, more robust woman like the others in camp. She was anything but that. Her chest was flat; her body pencil thin. I learned later she was fifty-two, but she might have been seventy. She walked up to us, smoothing back her long, graying hair and wiping her hands in a blue-checked apron. She was wearing lightweight shoes rather than boots, a plaid wool skirt, and sweater.

"This is my mammy," said one of the boys, and then turning to his mother, "Look at the cat!"

We glanced at each other over their heads. A cluster of

religious medals hung from a safety pin on her chest; a pierced earring dangled from one ear—the other ear had been ripped. Her eyes were a calm blue-gray, the right one flecked with brown. She must have been attractive once; beneath the web of wrinkles and small white scars was a faded beauty. She looked down at the kitten.

"Ah, he's beautiful," she said. Her voice was deep and raspy. "Is he a Persian?"

I wondered a second at the question, alert for signs of ridicule. But she only looked at the kitten, an ordinary tabby, and stroked it.

"What's his name?"

"Hillary."

"Hillary." She repeated the name with difficulty, then looked up and smiled through three thin decaying teeth. "He's going to be big. He looks like a very clever cat."

I smiled involuntarily at the absurd, yet sincere flattery. She then told me about Minnie, her own black cat, and how she loved it and how it caught rats as big as small dogs. One of the boys ran off to find Minnie. We continued to talk as waves of heat rose from the blacktop on which the trailers sat and bits of broken glass and scrap metal glinted in the sunlight. We talked about the weather ("grand"), and about America ("big"), and about how many sons and daughters she had had ("eighteen").

"Eighteen?" Doubt flickered across my mind, followed by a spasm of dismay; she's not lying, is she? I hoped not, since I had immediately liked her and had already had my fill of tall tales told by Travellers testing the gullibility of a young outsider. But Nan did have eighteen children, including three who had died.

Several years after that first meeting, I decided to write the story of Nan's life.[9] By that time I had finished my fieldwork with Travellers, having lived for a year with my husband, George, in a horse-drawn wagon parked next to Nan's trailer. During that time, Nan became my closest "informant" and friend—half teacher, half student. She had the advantage of age and experience, while I had had an education and opportunity.

Like most Travellers, Nan lacked pretense. She talked about her life and the lives of others—including details that made me cringe inwardly—in a matter-of-fact way, brushed with humor. She saw the irony of life, as many Irish do. But unlike many, she could also stand apart from Traveller culture and see both its virtues and follies.

Travellers' lives are filled with change and unexpected events, and Nan's story took twists and turns I never anticipated even though I knew her well. What emerged is not uniquely a Traveller story, although Nan was a Travelling person. Nor is it exclusively an Irish story, although she lived in Ireland most of her life. Neither is it solely a woman's story. It is a human story, filled with adversity and adventure, cruelty and compassion, sorrow and humor, bad luck and good.

Nan's spirit survived the tragedy of her life. Her greatest flaws were also some of her greatest strengths. To the end, she remained impulsive, trusting, and kind.

I I

The Sweep's Daughter

Nan was born in 1919 on All Soul's Day—a day devoted to prayer for the dead.[10] It was a cold, wet November day and a prophetic one given the way her life had gone. She was born "under a bush," as she described it, on the roadside outside Granard, a small village deep in the Irish Midlands. Nan's mother was camped in a tent with the older children and her own mother. Nan's father was serving in the British Army.

Granard is known throughout the Midlands as "the back of beyond"; its people described as "mean," spiritless, and lacking in "devilment," that most desired of Irish traits. In November, the reputation seems deserved. Even the landscape is dull and monotonous. Gray and green are everywhere, from the stone walls and tangled hedgerows that divide the flat boggy land to the dark sky and slate roofs of every home. Constant wetness imparts an air of melancholia and decay. Cows huddle together in ankle-deep water; crows drop from dripping wires to scream unexpectedly at ear height, while ivy silently strangles the trees. In a tent it was miserable.

Nan's mother, Sarah Power, was the daughter of Pat Power, a "wireworker" from county Waterford who walked the roads making and selling wire plant holders and umbrella stands. Nan's grandmother, Oney Ward, was an accomplished story teller who came from one of the oldest tinsmithing families on the road.[11] Nan's father, John Donohoe, was a chimney sweep by trade—as had been his father and grandfather—but like many poor Irishmen of his day, he had joined the British Army.[12] While serving as a gunner with the 47th Regiment in France, shrapnel penetrated his right hand and he never regained its full use. His nerves and sight were never quite the same either, and when he returned from the war, he was forced to hire help to climb out onto the roofs of the "Big Houses" whose chimneys he swept. Because his mother had been the daughter of a settled laborer, other Travellers always referred to him as "John, the *buffer*"—their word for a non-Traveller or country person.

Ireland in 1919 was a rural society. Little had changed in generations. A small Protestant landlord class—the families of the "Big House"—balanced precariously atop a social pyramid made up of Catholic farmers and shopkeepers, and at the base of it all, great numbers of landless poor: laborers, cottiers, and Travelling People. At the time of Nan's birth, 700 years of British rule were finally coming to an end; the "Troubles"—Ireland's war of independence and subsequent civil war—had broken out two months before.[13] But children are often oblivious to such things, and besides, by 1923 when the civil war was over, Nan was only three years old. Her only memory of those years is of a much more significant event. It happened on a winter Sunday.

"I was only young, but still I remember it, Sharon," Nan told me as we sat at the campfire one day.

WE WERE climbing up the hill to go to mass. It was snowing and me mother held me by the hand. On the ground a big handbag was lying open. Me mother picked it up and inside all this shopping money was tied up in a bundle. Me mother didn't know who owned it, so she gave it in to the priest, and the priest read it off the altar. Well, it belonged to a very rich woman in the town. And what do you think she—a rich woman—gave me mother? A half crown. The old half crown with the horse on it. Two and six it was worth. Me mother wouldn't take it. It was insulting. She told the priest, "Let her keep that, Father. You may give it back to her."

Me mother was expecting a pound. The woman could have given her a pound. We were all small then, and a pound would buy an awful lot. I'll never forget that bag nor I'll never forget me mother. I think she was talking about it before she died—the meanness of it.

Poor Granard—dull and mean.

The following year, Nan's parents moved to nearby Edgeworthstown—shortened to "Edgerstown" in speech—an unpretentious market town with a wide main street, wide enough in Nan's day to accomodate herds of cattle and carts on market day. The town is much the same today. The people of Edgeworthstown seem not to have changed either. Strangers are still greeted with silent stares. A question is still met with caution and curiosity: "Who are ye looking for? . . . Who did ye say ye were looking for?" persisted a woman with opaque eyes and a black stain the length of her front teeth. I had asked directions to Church Street, where Nan's family had lived. But she wasn't prepared to tell me without knowing more. Perhaps this was why Nan's family used to sneak out of their house when they left the town to travel each spring.

WE USED to love for me father to leave the house to travel, Sharon. We never used to go till March—till St. Patrick's Day. "I wish to God it was the seventeenth of March, Paddy's Day, when the stones turn in the water," me father'd say. The people used to believe that on Patrick's Day the stones turned over in the water and then the cold went out of the winter. We all believed that. I think the country people believe it yet. "Oh, I wish to God it was Patrick's Day so I can get off to get me few pounds," he'd say, and he'd be thinking of sweeping his chimneys.

And a couple of days before Patrick's Day, he'd pull out his chimney sticks and he'd bundle them up and have them ready. He'd go down and get his little donkey and his harness and have everything ready for the day. The night before, he'd come to us in bed and say, "Now don't sleep in, children, in the morning." And he'd be up at five before the neighbours would be up and away with him. And we'd be gone out in front of him; me mother wouldn't be seen walking through Edgeworthstown following a donkey and cart. She didn't want the neighbours to see us and say, "Look there! They're leaving now. Look at the tinkers." So we'd get up early and sneak off. Me father would tell us where we were going to move, and we'd be there in front of him. The neighbours would know we were gone when they'd get up and see the lock, the big old-fashioned lock, on the door.

Me father had different call-backs. Maybe one woman would want her house done in March—all her chimneys swept—another one in April. Me father had to keep travelling around. The farmers loved to see him coming. "I wish Donohoe was around. The chimney is smoking, and we can't put on a pot," they'd say. They kept the work for me father. They wouldn't have a strange sweep, only their own man that they had coming for years. Me grandfather and great-grandfather, they were all sweeps. Well, me father would have that contract every year. They trusted him; they'd leave the whole house under him.

A sweep had to be honest because he'd be coming into parlours, different bedrooms, and all their stuff would be there—jewellery, the very valuable stuff, money, and different things. The whole house was left under the sweep.

It was a very early job. Me father would be up at five in the morning. There were some jobs where he'd have to do all the chimneys in the house. There was a Captain Grant

near Loughnavalley, that's about eight miles from Mullingar
on the Ballymahon road. He was very good to me father on
account of knowing him for years and me father being an
ex-serviceman. This Captain Grant had an awful big house—
"Rathconrath"—and me father used to go every year to
clean the chimneys. He wouldn't do it all in the one day. It
was a very big place. And some of the chimneys when he
couldn't clear them, he'd have to climb up to the top of the
roof to do them right. When he was young, me father could
climb, but the war affected his nerves. So he'd get one of
me brothers—Pat, Willie, or John—or a neighbour's son to
help him. But it was a very dirty job. Willie didn't like the
soot, and John, the Lord have mercy on him, he wouldn't do
it, either.

We travelled by donkey and cart. We wouldn't rush goin'.
We'd stay here and there, different parts of the road to let
the donkey rest. It took about a week to get to Mullingar
from Edgeworthstown, about twenty mile away. When me
father went sweeping, he'd take the donkey or he'd walk—
he'd just carry his sticks on his shoulder and walk. He
couldn't ride a bicycle because of the effects of the war. And
when he got older, after me brothers were gone, he'd get a
bus.

He had different size sticks: five-foot rods, six-foot rods,
and even eight-foot rods. The weight of them to carry! And
he had a big bag to catch the soot and a small handbrush for
sweeping that up and two sizes of brushes in case there'd
be any bends in the chimney, and different small brushes to
take down birds' nests. Then he had a scraper to scrape
down the chimney. He'd carry all that on this shoulder, the
same as if it were nothing.

While her father was out, Nan walked to the neighboring
cottages and farms with her mother who carried scrubbing
brushes, lace, needles, boot polish, and camphor balls in a

basket over her arm. These she sold or bartered for potatoes, turnips, eggs, bacon, homemade bread and butter, and even flour, sugar, and salt. Sometimes she was given cast-off clothing and shoes as well, but she never viewed these handouts as charity. Travellers were an integral thread in the intricate fabric of rural Irish life. It was their due.

Besides, Nan's mother also brought stories and news to the women she visited, providing welcome relief from the routine and isolation of farm life. Other Travellers made tinware, recast legs on broken pots, sold dishware, cleared ditches, repaired fencing and out-buildings, thinned beet, pulled potatoes, and bought and sold donkeys and horses. Not every Travelling family provided all these services, but it is likely that most had tried them at some time. Nan's father once sold well water from a churn he carried on the back of his donkey cart through the streets of Longford: a penny a bucket.

Nan's job was to carry the "sweet can"—the three-quart container in which they collected buttermilk for making bread and cakes. She was a good girl but absent-minded, the rapt occupant of a vivid and private mental world. And she had two great weaknesses: flowers and pets.

ME MOTHER had terrible trouble with me, Sharon. But I couldn't help it; I had to do it. If we were going up to a Big House, I'd wait a bit behind her, and then coming back along the avenue, I'd rob the flowers. I'd take a flower here and a flower there. I'd put them down under me cardigan and hide them till we'd get miles away. I'd do that every day I'd go out with me mother. "Where are you getting the flowers?" she'd say. "I don't see anyone giving them to you."

"Oh, the woman . . . I went in after you came out, and she gave me the flowers," I'd say.

We'd go back to camp then, and I'd put them in a jam jar with water and keep them there for days. We might be three weeks stopping in the one place or maybe only a week. The flowers would be dead when we'd be moving, so I'd go out and get more. Many a slap in the face I got over the flowers. "I'm watching you going up this avenue and if you touch this lady's flowers, I'll kill you coming down," me mother'd say. Still, maybe there'd be one flower I'd really like. And if I didn't get that flower, I'd be thinking about it all day.

Me mother told a priest about me once, "Funny thing Father, Nan's grand but—"

"We like Nan," the priest said. "She's a very good girl and she's great at her prayers." He was a nice priest that knew us.

"But Father," me mother said, "you don't know anything about her. She's always robbing." I got afeard when she told the priest I was always robbing.

"Oh, I don't believe she's always robbing," he said. "Why, Nan's too good to rob."

"No Father," me mother said. "She's always robbing flowers. No matter how I beat her, it's no good."

"Well," he said, "there's something good in her if she's fond of flowers. There's something good."

I used to think of that after. How I heard that priest tell me mother that there's something good in me. Even today, Sharon, I think of what I heard the priest say to me mother. But be God, there was nothing at all good in me, not one thing good. I was always saying after, "That priest made a big mistake with me." I never was lucky. Even from the time I was small, I never was lucky.

One day I went with me mother to a farmer's house in Borahill, not far from where we lived in Edgeworthstown, and there was a big pig in the shed. It was a big old sow with all her little young pigs. Oh, they were lovely. Well, this farmer's wife was good to me mother; she used to give me mother anything she'd want. So me mother went in to the cottage, and they sat talking about all the neighbors. "The

MacGreines got their potatoes in now, Mrs. Donohoe," the farmer woman would say.

"Ah, God bless them," me mother'd say.

"And they kilt a pig. Go down there now, Mrs. Donohoe. They kilt a pig, and you'll get the liver or something."

"I will," said me mother.

I stayed out to watch the little pigs and I wouldn't go away from them. So the woman stepped outside the door and said, "That old sow will et you! Don't go in a-near that shed because she'll et you." But the old sow didn't mind me, and I was even picking up her little pigs.

When me mother and the woman came out, I went over to me mother and said, "Ask her. Ask her would she give me one. Ask her!"

"And how would you rear one," said this woman, "if you got it?"

"Oh, I'd feed it bread, milk, everything," I said.

"Well, the next time you come round, I'll give you one of these little sows. It's only two or three days old now," she said.

"When will I come?"

"Come next week." But wasn't she only saying that to get me out of the shed.

Well, I went home then and I was thinking and thinking about the little pig. I couldn't sleep. I could hardly eat. The next week came and me mother sent me on to the woman next door to where the pigs was. This woman used to give me mother lovely clothes. "And the woman next door is giving you the little pig," me mother said. Didn't she want to coax me to go and get the clothes.

"All right, I'll go," I said. So back I goes.

I was in getting the clothes and eating some cake, when the farmer woman next door seen me and run into her cottage. She knew I'd be after the little pig. So when I got all me things, I went over to her door and shouted, "I seen you, Missus."

"Oh Nan," she said. "You needn't come in now because me husband is not here. Next week I'll give the pig to you."

"Are you sure now? Promise me you will!" But I was real angry.

Me mother used to go once a week or maybe twice or three times a month to them houses. "Will you come with me today, Nan?" she said about a week later.

"Which way are you going?"

"I'm going that way, and you can come and maybe the woman will give you the little pig," she said. Well, I was getting sick of being promised this little pig. But on we comes anyway. When me mother got to the house she said, "God bless you." And in we went.

After I ate me fill, I said, "Mother, I'll be going home on in front of you."

"Oh, don't go home now, Nan," she said. "Wait. I want you to carry some things."

"I'll wait down the road," I said. "I'm going on to that other house." There was a young girl in the house below, and she used to give me a lot of rings and brooches and dolls. I was terrible for dolls.

"Well, wait down there until I go down," me mother said.

"I will." But in I sneaks into the neighbor woman's shed and stole one of the little pigs. And away with me. I was that vexed. "Now," said I, "she won't laugh at me."

About a mile away from the house, I took the little pig and me mother's can of buttermilk and with the lid of the can I kept feeding the pig and he swelled himself drinking the can of buttermilk. He was only a young pig with lovely silky skin. I put the lid on the can then and hid the pig under me coat.

Me mother caught up with me, "Did you get the things from your woman?"

"She wasn't at in," I said. "You needn't go near the cottage." Sure, I hadn't gone in at all; it was the pig I'd gotten.

We started walking home. But I wouldn't walk with me

mother, because she'd hear the pig grunting, grunting, grunting. It was grunting all the time. So I kept behind her.

"Come on, Nan. Your father will kill me if I'm not home early. He'll be starving with the hunger and he won't make his own tea," she said. "Hurry on. He'll be starving with the hunger."

"You keep going," I said. "Me shoe is cutting me."

"Take off your shoe and run in your bare feet."

"No, I won't."

She'd go on a bit and then she'd stand and call me, "Wait till I get you home. I'll hit you a beating." But I made out me foot was paining me, and when she got far enough ahead, I went into the bushes, across under the ditch, and tied the poor pig's legs to the bushes with a bit of me petticoat. I left the pig there and went on.

When I got back, me mother was sitting down at the camp making tea, real happy. Then she started in washing her hands. And she got a big spoon and her big dish for making bread. "Nan, get me that can with the buttermilk," she said.

"I think I see something," I said, and I ran down the road for me life. I could hear her screaming at me but I made out to be deaf. There was a river and I went down and played with the stones at the river.

Next thing me father came up, "Did you hear your mother calling you?"

"No," said I, "I didn't."

"Come here you," he said, and he caught me be the plaits and nearly pult me hair off me head. "Get up there. Your mother wants you. Where's the buttermilk?" Me father didn't like the idea of no bread.

"I didn't want to tell her but I spilt it on the road," I said.

"Don't tell lies."

"I did. I spilt it on the grass, that's why she couldn't see it." I used to make up terrible lies.

Well, I had to run three miles to a farmer's house to get

more buttermilk. There was a hole in me shoe and me feet were killing me from the stones of the road.

The next morning I got up early and fixed a little place with a bit of straw under the pig and stole bread and gave it to the pig. I was back in camp when this farmer came down the road. He was in a rage. I looked up and he was about six foot—a big tall skinny man. And if he ever hit me father—me father was only a small man—he'd of kilt him.

"Are you there, John Donohoe?" asked the farmer.

"I am, Mr. Egan."

"Where's your wife?"

"I'm here, Mr. Egan," me mother said. "What's wrong with you?"

"Weren't you at my house yesterday?"

"I was," she said.

"Well, I didn't think you'd ever do such a thing."

"What's wrong with you?" said me father. He was very hot-tempered.

"I'll let you know, Jack, in a minute," said the farmer. He was that vexed, he called me father Jack. "Why did you go in and steal my pig?" he said to me mother.

Me mother couldn't answer. She knew then that I took him but she was afraid to tell me father because she knew he'd kill me in the morning with the strap. "Ah, God bless us and save us," she said. And she went into all the prayers in the world about the little pig. "The little pig must have sneakin' out or maybe one of the poor neighbors, the poor half-starved fellas in the cottages done it. What would I do with a pig?" she said. "Don't you know Travelling People wouldn't have a pig."

"Well, have it or not, it's gone," he said, "and I'm going for the guards. None of my pigs was ever harmed before. And you were reared around here. I'm surprised at you doing a thing like this, John."

"Me wife said she didn't do it," said me father. "Will you cool down!" He done everything he could because he was very nervous of the guards. Me father was a very honest man but if his name went on the papers and he sweeping with all the quality around, he'd be ruined. "Right!" said me father. "I'm going to the guards meself now, for me character and me wife's character."

Me mother called me over, "Come here, Nan."

"What?" I said.

"You took the little pig. Give it to me and I'll hand it back to the man."

I started roaring then, "I'm not giving me pig! I'm not giving me pig!"

"What's this about the pig?" said me father.

"Nan has it." Me mother had to tell him then.

"Nan, did you take him?" me father said. "I'll give you a beating you'll never forget."

The farmer looked at me and he felt sorry then. "Oh," he said, "I understand now. Come here and show me."

"I won't show you," I roared and I took off running through the fields. Me father sent me brother Willie out after me, and he caught me and held me. On comes me father then with his army belt and three straps he give me of this belt, right across the legs and I tore with briars and all.

"Show me where the pig is," he said.

"All right, I'll show you," I said. "Don't touch me no more." And I took them to the pig. I had the pig in a lovely little hole with straw.

When the farmer seen it, he got sorry. "Don't beat her anymore, John."

Me father got sorry too. "How much is the pig," he said. A pig was only cheap that time.

"I'd give her the pig, John, but it won't live. The pig is too young. It'd die with her," the farmer said.

"It wouldn't," I said. "It et the bread and me mother's can of buttermilk."

"Oh no!" yelled me mother. "I never washed the can. I'm going to kill you altogether now."

I did get kilt the next morning. Me father was like that. He wouldn't beat you right away if you done anything bad. He'd be real sneaky. He'd smile and let you go to bed, then at six in the morning he'd let you have it. I never forgot that beating and I never will. I was nine year old.

I think it was a week after, me father was out cleaning chimneys in a cottage and he was telling this woman about what I'd done with the pig. Travellers always talked when they'd be doing anything. "I'll give you something for her now," the woman said. "A bantam." So on comes me father home.

"Nan, I got you a lovely little pet," he said.

"What'd you get me?"

"A little bantam. You forget about that dirty old pig. You'd never have reared him. We couldn't look after it in the house in winter because he'd have growing too big."

I hadn't thought of that; I thought that time the pig would always keep small.

Well, I was pleased with this little bantam. It was a beauty and ever so small. Every day I'd go out into the fields where there'd be young oats and tear the tops off the oats and throw them in to the little hen. And she started to lay eggs, and the little eggs was so small.

One day me father said, "An old friend of ours has come to camp with us." She was a first cousin of me father—a widow woman with a bad leg—he always took her out for a couple weeks in the summer.

"It couldn't be that you're rearing bantams!" she said as soon as she saw me pet.

"A little bantam is no harm," said me mother, "it's Nan's pet." But Travelling People that time didn't like the idea of bantams. They thought that if a bantam crowed at night, after twelve o'clock, that something would go wrong. And that if a hen crowed, there'd be trouble.

So after that, me brother Joe told me, "Nan, you'd better watch your bantam or they'll do away with her."

We were staying out by Gaybrook. It was a big wood, a lovely place but lonesome at night. And what happened, Sharon? Up gets me bantam about one o'clock in the morning and starts crowing. Only the way I cried meself sick saved her: they had to let me keep her.

"We'll leave it," said me mother. "If I done away with that bantam, Nan would go mad." But she blessed herself a hundred times that day.

In the afternoon, they yoked up the pony and cart—me brother John, me father, me mother, and our friend. "Come on," said John. "I'll bring you to the fair." There was a fair in Mullingar. Me brother had a great trotting mare, very fast, and he loved to get a good drive with this mare. So they climbed into the cart and away with them all into Mullingar. None of us children used to be allowed into fairs. Me father never liked the idea of bringing children into town.

Well, they got their few bottles of stout and they were coming on home at night on this big lonely road. They were going along singing, when the wind came up strong and something hopped out of the ditch—a newspaper or a white bit of cloth on a dark road. And didn't the pony freckin' [get frightened] and away goes the pony in a runaway. The next thing, the harness broke and the pony run right out from under the cart, and they were all thrown out on the side of the road. Me brother's arm was broke. The old woman—the poor crayture—her face and her arms was all scrapped. And the rest of them had bruises all over them. They were miles from Mullingar and they couldn't catch the pony. But for the luck of God, a man passed them going home. I believe the moans and curses coming out of them were terrible. And he gathered them up and brought them back to Mullingar hospital and got them dressed.

We were sitting up waiting for them, wondering what had kept them. "They got drunk or they met friends," we said and we were happy enough and went to bed and didn't

bother with it anymore. Near morning here they come all in
bandages, and John with his arm in plaster. The very minute
they landed, we got up and made them a cup of tea. Then
they all went to lay down for an hour.

But when they got up: "Where's that bantam? Where's that
bantam? It's not lucky. It's not right to keep a bantam hen
that's crowing. Nan can cry anyway she likes this time, she's
not lucky, with the red hair on her. She and her bantam are
crying bad luck at us." A red-haired girl they used to count
as unlucky. They didn't pass any heed about boys, but if a
girl had red hair, it was bad luck. "She's not lucky, that red
one. She's crying us away, her and her pets," they said.

Well, when I heard about me bantam, I said to meself, I
hope to God me bantam won't move. There was a tree up
overhead, a big white-thorn bush. We had a fire under it,
and the little bantam was roosting up in the top of the
bushes.

"Where's that bantam?" said me father. He had his sweeping stick—the one with the big metal screw on the top—in
his hand. Oh, I said to meself, me poor little bantam is dead
if he gets a clout of that. I didn't know what to do and I
started crying.

They looked everywhere, up and down, and couldn't find
the bantam. But the very next morning the poor little thing
started crowing. "There it is," said me mother. "There's the
unlucky bantam. Get it quick! It's a devil. Get it away from
us." Me father went up with the stick and broke the little
bantam's head.

"He's dead now. He's dead!" I cried, catching it be the
legs. And I pult it in the bushes and tried to hide it. The
poor little thing crawled and crawled for about an hour
after. But they had killed it. Every pet I used to get, there
was something wrong with it.

I was always unlucky.

"We were always kept going, Sharon," Nan told me as we huddled in front of the small coal stove in her trailer. It was raining outside and steam covered the windows.

THERE WAS eleven of us living—Lizzie, John, Mary, Pat, Willie, Joe, Chrissie, Eileen, Maggie, Angela, and me. Me parents always kept us busy. We'd get up in the morning and the first thing we'd have to do was get a dish of water and soap and get out and wash ourselves. We'd have a pot of stirabout then—the oaten meal. And then one or two of us would go on with me mother selling or begging to a few farmers. Some of the girls would stay home to tidy the camp. Those that were old enough would bake bread, and they'd have the dinner boiled when she come home. The boys would cut timber for the fire or bring water so the girls could do the cleaning and cooking. Then they'd be off with me father and the donkey, always with me father. And me sister Lizzie, the Lord have mercy on her, she followed me father everywhere.

We never had many games to play. The boys used to get horseshoes and fire them along the grass on the side of the road. The girls played skittles. We'd get bits of wood, cut them out like little soldiers with a knife, and put them standing. Which ever of us knocked the most over would win the game. But what we used to play most was spinning tops. We all had little tops and whips. The girls were just as bad as the boys for those tops. And we had chalk for marking and skipping.

Sometimes a bunch of us would sneak away and go down to a farmer's field and jump all around in the cocks of hay. We'd do it for fun. But in the morning the farmer would be up to the camp roaring and screaming about his hay. Me father, and every other Travelling man, would have to go down and tidy up the cocks of hay or maybe spend the whole day working with the farmer to keep him from going to the guards. We used to be beat to death then over the hay. But we had no other games to play.

It used to be lovely years ago, Sharon, when a crowd of
Travellers would be together. That time they'd love to get
together for company. After their work was done, they'd sit
around the fires. The men would go off and talk men's
talk—about swaps of horses or deals they done or what they
might be making. The women would sit at the fire and gab-
ble about children, their sons, or maybe what they were
begging all day. The children would be playing round the
place; some of us would sit listening. But if we laughed, me
mother used to run us. We never was allowed to laugh at me
mother or to laugh among ourselves while she was talking.

One night I was sitting in the door of the tent sewing and
listening to me mother and this other woman chatting. Maggie had two little boys—Johnnie and Tommie. They were
out on the road throwing stones. They'd put up a bottle or
an old tin and they'd fire stones at it.

"Look at this shot, Johnnie," said Tommie.

"Now, Tommie, watch," said Johnnie.

"Yes, Johnnie."

"Come on, Tommie."

"Can you do this, Johnnie?"

The way they were talking almost drove me mother mental: "That's a funny way your boys go on, Maggie," she said.

"Don't mind them, Sarah," Maggie said. So me mother
forgot about them. She had her clay pipe—all the old people that time used to smoke them—and she was puffing
away, having a lovely chat, when Johnnie let go of this stone.
And didn't it hit me mother a belt in the mouth and put her
pipe up in the air in a hundred pieces. Well, she lifted a big
burning stick from the fire and jumped up and shook it at
them. "Well, Johnnie and Tommie," she said, "I'm going to
put you running." She went to run for them but didn't her
long skirt trip her up and she fell over the shafts of the cart
down against the ground. Her guts nearly fell out. Well,
Sharon, if you heard me mother roar.

Me father run to her. "Where are you, Sarah?" he said.

The poor man was half blind from the war. "What's wrong with you?"

"I'm here," she said, and she lifted the sweet can of tea and hit him in the forehead. I needn't tell you all the names she started calling him. "What class of company do you have me in with?" she roared. "The dirty company you mix me up with? And bring me poor children out here! Look at that! Me pipe! What sort of people are they?" Me father stood washing the tea leaves off his face.

"That's terrible swearing, Sarah, frontinst the poor children," he said.

Johnnie and Tommie didn't wait no more. They flew out into the farmer's field, into the cocks of hay. Me mother runned after them but she couldn't catch them. When she got back she said to me father, "I'm sorry, *a vock.*"[14] That's the way they used to talk. "I'm sorry now over those little gossoons," she said. They called boys gossoons then. "I'm sorry about saying that about those poor little gossoons. Now, Jaunty *a vock,*" she said. "What will I do for a pipe?"

"I don't know," said me father. "Why don't you smoke your thumb."

"Now Jaunty," said me mother, "there's a pub up the road. It's about a mile away, and I have the price of a couple of pints. I'll give it to you if you let me get one draw out of your pipe." Me father smoked a brier root pipe, but he was very fussy about it; he wouldn't give his own father a smoke out of that pipe.

"Not with your ugly mouth," he said. "Not for twenty pound would I give you a draw of me pipe."

Me mother was in an awful hobble then. She got up, put on her shawl, and walked to some old farmer's house, about four miles in through the fields. All the old farmers used to keep a few clay pipes; the shanks would be broken off them. You only had to tip a clay pipe and it'd break. So she went on and came back with a little bit of a pipe. "I wish to God tomorrow would come," she said. "I'll get off this road and into a shop." You could buy a clay pipe for a hapenny then. We laughed for a month over that.

As the days shortened and the nights turned cold each year, Nan's family returned to Edgeworthstown. A mantle of inactivity draped rural life in the winter. It was the slack season for farmers and consequently, there was little work for Travellers to do. So most settled down, occupying abandoned "waste" houses in the countryside or renting cheap cottages in town.

Nan's family was especially glad to return home the winter of 1930. The summer and autumn had been unusually wet. Their tent had been washed away in a sudden rain; Nan's father had pitched it on low ground. Following that, her mother chose their campsites. The whole cycle of farm life had been off balance. Incessant rain the previous winter had made field preparation difficult; sowing had been a month behind schedule; and as soon as the oats and potatoes had been planted, harsh winds and rain returned. Potatoes rotted in the ground; cut turf stayed sodden. The farmers were irritable and had less to give. By November, Edgeworthstown beckoned in more ways than one.

While the Donohoe's had been traveling, power poles had been erected in the streets of town and on the evening of November 7, current from the Shannon hydroelectric scheme was switched on. Nan's family could now see from one end of the main street to the other at night. The more privileged, who could afford electricity in their homes, saw the darkest corners of their rooms for the first time.

"It was a little house, Sharon," Nan told me as she got up to open the trailer door. A refreshing rush of cold air came in; rain was still pounding on the roof and pavement outside.

THEY WERE all little houses. When you'd walk in the door, there was a front room. All the people in Edgeworthstown made kitchens out of it because there was no other kitchen. And there was a little front parlour. Me mother made a bedroom for herself and me father out of that. There was two rooms upstairs. One was a double room for the girls. There was three beds in that room. If anyone came to visit or stay with us, we would share. We'd put a partition up—a curtain—and make two rooms. The boys had their own room, the back one.

Me mother always kept a spare mattress underneath one of the beds in case any poor stranger—a poor old man or woman—came looking for lodging. Some of them would be making from Mullingar to Longford, begging their way. Me mother'd bring the mattress down and put it beside the fire and make them a drop of tea. Me father used to always tell us, "Always have the kettle boiling. You never know what poor person might come to the door of a winter night for a cup of tea. Never let anyone sleep out if you have any shelter at all. Always shelter them."

Me father had a pension from the British Army, and the British Legion used to help us out. They'd give all the children clothes every quarter until we were fourteen. Me father never had to borrow. He could go to any shop in Edgeworthstown and get anything he wanted on credit, his word.

There was a big shop at the corner with a little metal pump outside it. One part of it was a grocery and one part a pub. And there was Farrell's. They had a pub and a grocers too. They had everything. Me father'd get a bag of turf and he'd pay a young fella to bring the logs in. And he'd pack up big fires. Me mother's pots was always boiling and she'd bake her own bread because some of the boys wouldn't eat loaf bread—the store bread. We were very well fed.

We were reared tender but strict. When I was small, I didn't swear in front of me mother and father or in front of any old Travelling Person. If I did, I'd get an awful slap across the face. And we weren't allowed to smoke, none of us. Me father used to wear a cap and the peak of it would cut you to pieces. He'd give it to you in the ears or maybe across the back of the neck. And if you took anything or stole anything and he caught you, he'd say, "Oh, that's lovely. Where did you get it?" Then he'd take you right to where you got it and in front of the person, he'd thrash you. And in the morning, there'd be the army belt. He'd never hit you with it around the head, but your legs'd be a rainbow of colors. After, he'd be sorry. "I didn't want to hit you," he'd tell you. "I'm sorry now. But if you ever do that again. . . ."

Me father was softer on me than on the rest. Sometimes he wouldn't touch me, he'd warn me. But I'd still venture it.

My parents were very religious and hardworking. They didn't believe in swearing, though they did. And they believed in going to church every Sunday, though they didn't. But the children had to go. "Out!" We could be dying with flu or anything and still we had to get out. At night me father would throw himself on his knees at the fire and he'd take the rosary beads and we'd answer him. You'd have to answer him. And they got every one of us to school.

I was surprised when Nan told me this, since it was unusual for Travelling children to go to school. Two weeks of religious instruction in order to make their confirmation was the most education many received; families would camp near a convent and send their children to the nuns. But Nan attended the convent school in Ballymahon, a pretty village on the River Inny ten miles south of Edgeworthstown. Her eldest sister, Lizzie, had married a poor laborer from nearby Ballynacragy, and they had moved to Ballymahon, Nan's mother's home village. Nan lived with them on and off for a couple of years. She was company and helped Lizzie with the baby. Her absence from home also eased the burden on their parents. But in time Nan got lonely and returned to Edgeworthstown, attending school sporadically along with her younger brothers and sisters.

"I was backward," Nan explained simply.

I COULDN'T learn much; the only thing I could get quick was Irish. I hated the idea of school and I was always sort of wild. I'd go out playing all day or walking through the fields, pulling flowers. I'd be there for hours, sitting down or walking around. Anything to keep away from school, because I was a bad mixer. There'd always be some of the kids picking on me, calling me "tinker." You know the way children goes on. And I was very hot tempered. If they said anything, there'd be fighting. I had a couple of friends in the school but I got fed up and wouldn't go at all.

I used to stay home to help me mother, and she teached me me prayers and catechism. Me mother and her mother before her always got their own children teached—how to get their communion, how to receive, what to say, and all like that. I'd be washing up or making a cup of tea, and me mother'd tell me what to say. I used to listen and I had it off by heart. The school master said to me mother once, "Mrs. Donohoe, your child didn't come in for her teaching."

"Ah, don't mind her," me mother said. "She'll be teached."

Before I was to get me confirmation, me mother went round to different ladies she knew in town and they gave her clothes. Everyone in Edgeworthstown thought getting confirmed a great thing. I had three or four confirming suits. The banker's wife gave me a lovely dress with roses on it, but I wore a plain dress—the one I picked meself—a plain white dress with a little bit of lace. I loved this dress and me white gloves, me white shoes and stockings, and me little handbag. And I picked a lovely hat, a straw hat with a rose on it. I thought it was beautiful.

Well, on we comes to the chapel, and the schoolmaster

was inside the door. That time when you were getting confirmed, you wore a little ribbon on your shoulder. If you were backward, didn't know so much, you'd get a white one. That way when the bishop would look at you, he'd let you off easy. And if you were great at your catechism, you'd get a blue one. On account of me not showing up for me teaching, the school master threw a white one on me right shoulder. One of the shopkeeper's daughters was standing beside me with her blue ribbon.

That time, the bishop would ask you a lot, not like now—one word or two. He'd keep you there a long time. And I was afeard on account of me parents telling me about the slap on the jaw the bishop was supposed to give you, so'd you'd know when you were confirmed. I had me face freezed waiting for this clout.

Well, the bishop started asking questions. Some of the children didn't know the words or maybe they did but they were too scared of the bishop with the big hat on to answer. But when he came to me, I shouted me answer out. "Oh, that's what I love," he said. "A person shouting it out. Good girl." And he asked me again. He kept at me then, and me mother was shaking at the back of the chapel with her heart thumping. But everything he asked me, I came out with it—straight out.

The bishop went on down along the line then, and some of them were so amazed with me, they couldn't hardly answer him. He put three of them back. Even the shopkeeper's daughter was sent back to the next year.

At the end, them all—the ladies, shopkeepers, and all—were coming up to me and giving me money. It was a small town and the chapel was overcrowded for confirming. They all shook hands with the schoolmaster. "Master, you did a right job with that one," they said.

"Nan, you were great," me mother said.

"Was I?"

"Oh, you were," she said. "You were great." I didn't care once I was confirmed. I was glad to get away from the bishop and I was peppering to get outside.

When spring came, Nan's family was "peppering" to return to the road. Her father had scores of chimneys to sweep after their heavy winter use. Her mother had a new basket of "swag" to sell. The Donohoes were a handsome family and well known in the district. They might beg, but they had dignity. Indeed, the landlord class referred to them as "nature's gentlemen." Travellers had a place in rural society and as long as they did not abuse the settled community's generosity, relations between the two were peaceful. This was especially true in the Midlands where the land was rich and the farming community properous.

WESTMEATH WAS a rich county, Sharon. The farmers had plenty of money. They'd buy a thing off me mother—a scrubbing brush, boot polish, a bit of lace—and give her full money. And we always got plenty of food. In every farmer's backyard was a big hole that they'd put their potatoes in to save them in winter. "Go out to the back, Mrs. Donohoe, and take a bucket of potatoes," they'd say. And we'd go into the fields and take a cabbage and turnips. And we never had to buy bacon, because the farmers cured their own. They'd kill their own pig and hang it up in the ceiling, in the rafters. And the farmers' wives used to churn their own butter and keep their own milk.

We never had to buy flour. Me mother would come along selling or begging and when she'd be going, she'd say to the farmer's wife, "Could I have a plate of your flour, God bless you." The farmer women always had a big sack of flour in the corner of the house over against the dresser where everyone could see it, and me mother used to carry her own white flour bag. Some of them would say, "Do you want all white flour, Mrs. Donohoe?" And they'd take a big dinner plate off the dresser and put down that big plate in the bag and take it full up. We'd go to three or two houses then and get the making of two cakes. We never ate much store bread, only homemade cake bread what me mother made or what the farmer women would give us. Some of the farmers was very good-hearted, they'd give us a bag of tea or sugar. Sure we had nothing to buy, only tobacco.

Still, there were complaints. Newspapers reported polluted wells, trampled crops, broken fencing, and stolen vegetables. And now and then there was a public outcry as when a General Eoin O'Duffy, the commander of the local Civic Guard, railed at a meeting of the Longford County Council about "the spectacle of small farms giving a half stone of potatoes to any able-bodied, muscular tinker who happens to stroll along." People were contributing, he maintained, "to the continued living of idle and dissolute lives by an unworthy class"; and he urged them to adopt a more "unbending attitude."

Nan's family was occasionally approached by hostile farmers. They in turn blamed the landless laborers whose lot was in many ways worse than their own. Many were unemployed. Those that did work for farmers were often treated harshly, toiling long hours for small wages. They lived in crude one-room cottages, their lives unrelieved by the freedom of the travelling life.

THEY WERE half starved in the cottages, Sharon. The husbands wouldn't be working, and they wouldn't have a good dinner but maybe once a week. And they were that poor, they wouldn't be able to get turf. They had no bog of their own and a lot of them wouldn't be able to buy it. Turf was very cheap when I was young; I think it was two and six for the full of a donkey's carload. It was for nothing. Well, they'd be praying for the Travelling People to move in. And when we did, that's when the robbing was done. The turnips and onions would be gone out of the gardens, the potatoes would be rooted up, and the trees was cut down. The farmers would come and blame us.

But everyone knew me mother and father. They knew me granny too—me mother's mother, the Lord have mercy on her. The farmers used to love to see old Mrs. Powers coming, especially if there was children sick. Me granny would tell them what to do. She had her own cures; she was gifted that way. And in a couple of days, their children would be right. The farmers counted me granny very lucky.

Me mother too. Once I got a cut of glass in me heel and me leg swelled. And what did me mother do? She got a whole load of snails and put them on top of a stone and down with another stone. It was brutal the way she done it, getting the snails alive and breaking them. When she got a lot, she shoved it into the cut. She kept getting snails and keeping them in the cut and in no time the leg and all the swelling went down. The snails dragged all the posion out.

I never remember me mother getting a doctor for anything. Unless we had pneumonia, cause there was an awful lot dying with pneumonia them days. I was very near dying meself with it.

It was raining and I was out playing with the kids, sweating. And didn't I leave the wet, damp clothes on and I got pneumonia. Me mother didn't think it was too bad. And I was that stubborn—"Oh, I'm all right." But it turned into double pneumonia and the next thing, I didn't know where I was.

Me father and mother took me to Mullingar hospital. Doctor Keylan was the doctor. The only cure—I'll never forget—was boiled lemons. The nurses left big jugs of lemon water with lumps of lemon in it by me bed. They'd bring it boiling and tell me to drink it hot or cold. And spoonfuls of brandy. And they sweated me. They put a woolen coat over me chest and lungs and tied it there with strings. I was very near going that time.

When I did get well, they kept me there. The little sister, Sister Anne, and the nurses liked me and they left me there on account of our being poor. They used to knit me clothes and hats; if I had been older, they would have given me a job in the hospital. And the patients used to give me sweets and cakes. I used to give me sweets to any poor woman—a labouring man's wife—or young children that no one was coming up to visit. There was rich patients too—farmers' wives and rich people from Westmeath. They'd say, "Get me a drink. Tell the nurse I want her. Tell the doctor . . ." And I'd get them water or I'd go to the nurses and bring them milk or whatever they wanted. And I'd go to the shops for them. There was a little shop across the road. They used to give me tips—a few pence or a penny. When I left, I had a little bag of pennies.

There was one woman I liked a lot. She was a very old woman. The old women had their own little ward. She used to pray there in her bed and when she'd leave down her beads, she'd tell me about her grandchildren, daughters, and different things—stories. I loved this old woman. I'd stay more with the old woman than with the young ones. I used to go to see her every day. The nurses let me bring her in milk. I'd go to the kitchen and I'd fill up a jug of milk and bring it out to her. And I'd sneak her a cup of tea. I wasn't allowed to make tea but the nurses liked me and I was real nice to them. They'd say, "Who are you making that tea for?"

"Ah, it's for an old woman. I'll sweep up for you and I'll wash the cups for you, if you let me take it," I'd say. And I'd get the old woman a cup of tea.

Well, this day I went to see her, and the nurse said, "You're not to go in there now. No, your friend is very sick and the doctors would be angry." So I waited till I got her gone and I watched the doctor and all going out of the ward and I sneaked in. I went over to her bed and she was barely able to speak, but still I could understand her.

"Get me a drink," she said. "God bless you." She tried to lift her poor hands, so I put my hands on top of them. They were cold. "God bless you now. Get me a drink," she said.

Another old woman called me over, "I hope you're not getting afraid. That's your friend, and God will give you the strength. She's dying."

I started shaking. I didn't know she was dying. Didn't I think she was just taking a change. I didn't understand about death that time. "You mustn't shake," the old woman said. "You liked her and she'll be praying for you when she goes to heaven. Don't leave her now. She needs you to wet her lips." So I kept her lips wet. She kept moving her lips. The next thing, a bubble sucked down into her mouth and no lips opened. I felt all shaking. She went off like a bird, no bother, and she speaking to me. She went off lovely.

The old woman was just gone, when the nurse came in. With the shock of it, she grabbed me shoulder and pegged me through the door. I cried and cried. I wanted to get home then. The nurse came out to me and told me she was sorry. And I went back to where the old woman was left out and prayed over her. There she was with her curcifix. She looked lovely. I didn't see no more of her then. Two days after, me mother came. The nurses had told the guards to find me parents and tell them I was discharged.

And with that, Nan's childhood was over.

I I I

The Kitchen Maid

"Just get out," Nan's father said one morning. "You're fourteen, it's time for you to do for yourself."[15] And the next thing Nan knew, she was on the train for Dublin, the scenery of the Midlands fast becoming a green blur in the distance. Her father had arranged for her to work with a draper [dry goods merchant] in Dun Laoghaire, an elegant Victorian resort on the coast south of Dublin. "We don't want anything belonging to you," he said at the station. "If you want to send your mother a souvenir or a couple of bob, send it. Just go on now." Nan's mother had stayed home, but warned her as she left, "Don't mix with people. Don't mix with anyone you don't know." And now Nan sat squirming, surrounded by strangers and "tormented with worry."

WHEN I got off at the station, Sharon, I was scared to death. I'd never seen a city—so many people or so much traffic. There was only Edgeworthstown, and in the summertime me father might take us in to Mullingar. Still I had no other choice, so I made me way out and got on a tram. There was all little trams that time in Dublin. They was something like small trains, with tracks and all, but slow—I could nearly walk as quick. And they were noisy. I got on one anyhow, and made me way to Dun Laoghaire.

When I got there, I enquired me way to the O'Leary's. I worked on then the whole seven days because I was living in the house, helping the mistress clean up—dusting, polishing, making beds, and all. But mostly I was looking after Michael, their little son, a three-year old. I used to take him out on walks, down to the pier of a Sunday to look at the ships. I got five shillings a week.

I had one friend, Annie. She was from the country too, some part of Kerry. She worked two doors above me doing general, the same as I did. Annie was a couple year in the place and could go to any part of the city. Sometimes she'd bring me in to see me uncle—me father's brother—who lived in Carmel Hall off Meath Street. But still, I didn't like the city. I was lonely and I was always nervous—I used to be very shy. I'd walk around and I'd think everybody was looking at me.

I worked for six months, then I went home. I went to a friend in Mullingar and then me father came and picked me up. It was mainly for the training I went. Me father wanted to get me a bit of learning, so's if I ever got another job, I'd know what to do. The O'Leary's learned me everything.

I was only six months home when me father got me another job from a lady outside Mullingar, Mrs. Grant. Me father was a great man. He was respectable, although he was poor, and he had great references. Mrs. Grant knew him on account of his sweeping her chimneys and being in the war with her husband, Captain Grant. They were quality people, big people. Mrs. Grant had sisters in England, and she got me and Willie jobs in Northamptonshire with her sister, Mrs. Howard Evans, and her husband, the Major. Willie was to learn to be a butler, and I was to be trained for whatever I was best for—a housemaid, a kichen maid.

Well, in the end I was a kitchen maid.

"Gretton was a small little village, Sharon," Nan continued. It was cool but sunny outside, and we were seated as usual at the campfire. Someone had found the front seat of a car while out scrap collecting and placed it by the fire. And I now reclined in comfort on my own divan as Nan fried sausages in a blackened pan.

IT WAS pure beautiful, all little cottages. "There was only about four shops in it—a post office, the butcher's, a draper's shop, not many. Major Evans was the biggest man there. He had an awful big house and a very big staff, and he used to give work to all the poor people of the village. He had little red-bricked lodges for the gardener, the chauffeur, and the grooms. They raised their own sheep—little black sheep—and butchered their own mutton. And they had all their own horses and black hunting dogs. And there was a lovely big lawn with a big chestnut tree right out in the middle and it spreaded so wide. We all used to go out—the staff—we'd be in our uniforms, and many's the photo we had taken.

When I travelled to Gretton over forty-five years later to retrace Nan's steps, the chestnut tree was gone. It had been struck down by lightning. But Gretton was still a lovely place— a cluster of honey-colored stone cottages perched on a high limestone ridge overlooking the Welland Valley, itself a checkered cloth of tan and green textured by the broad undulating ridges of remnant medieval fields. Housing estates, built after World War II and in the early 1970s, now spread out at the edge, but they have not disturbed the center. The village green still contains the stocks and whipping post that meted out justice long before Nan's day. A chimney sundail reminds one of a time when hours passed as silently as a shadow. And just a few minutes walk away stands Gretton House, a part Georgian, part neo-Jacobean jumble of steep, slated gables and stone mullioned windows, surrounded by manicured lawns. It is not surprising that Nan fell in love with it.

Nan shared an attic room on the south side of the house

with the under housemaid, a wardrobe separating their beds. She was seldom in her room, however, except to sleep. Most of her time was spent in the large tiled kitchen at the opposite end of the house and in its adjoining scullery where vegetables were cleaned and prepared. And many a trip she made across the hall and down the steep, well-scrubbed flight of stairs to the cold cellar with its black slate counters and ceiling meat hooks and to the heated greenhouses outside where grapes and other fruit were grown. The kitchen maid had the lowest rank of the household staff; she was the first up and the last in bed.

Nan's brother Willie spent most of his time in the butler's pantry shining the silver and plate, washing the china for the "front of the house," and looking after the setting, serving, and clearing of the dining room table. "William," as the family referred to him, was good-looking and well suited to be a butler, a job where appearance counted. But because Gretton House was not that large, he did a fair amount of other work; he was valet to the Master, kept the drawing and dining room fires burning, locked the doors and windows at night, and even did heavier and dirtier work like washing windows. On special occasions, the Evans hired a professionally trained butler, an older man from the village, to wait on guests. The family couldn't risk having Willie make one of the mistakes they routinely endured, like the watery mustard he once prepared, exclaiming when they protested, "Oh, I thought you wanted it to pour out of the jug."

Nan's work took place behind the scenes where mistakes were less critical.

AT FIRST when I didn't know me job so well, I'd get up an extra hour early to have it done unknownst. I was scared in case I wouldn't be able to do me work right. I was only showed what to do a couple of times and the fear was on me. First thing I had to do was clean me range—clean out me flues, get out the soot and all, and then polish it. I had black polish and I'd polish it over. I'd have to have the range so that you could see your face in it. Then I'd light it. Then I'd wash me hands and start at the kitchen table.

It was that big, twenty could sit around it. I'd scrub me table, scrub it as white as I could get it. It had to be spotless white! This was the cook's kitchen and you had to have the table shining like ivory. Then I'd get on me hands and knees and scrub me floors. This kitchen must have been the biggest kitchen in the world, with all black and white tiles. I used to get a little mat and put it under me knees. There was no cleaners or no electric work that time, not even a mop. It was all hand work and knee work, all scrubbing and polishing. I had to buy me own dusters and wash them out and have them spotless.

At seven o'clock I'd call me cook; she slept in a little room above the kitchen. I'd knock on her door and hand her in her cup of tea. Then I had to set the table for the breakfast. The cook'd write down what to leave out and she'd leave the little letter for me in the kitchen. But I didn't read and write, so Willie'd come to me in the morning. The little letter would be there, and he'd read it, and I'd leave out everything for the breakfast. Some mornings it'd be poached eggs. Different mornings, it'd be scrambled eggs and toast. All this carry on. I'd wait there in the kitchen then till the cook came down, and she'd tell me what to get ready for the breakfast. What pots or pans she needed.

At first, there was a scullery maid. But I only seen her a month and then she got out. After that I had to do the scullery maid's job and me own. I did all the vegetables. I'd peel the potatoes and have them ready; then I'd help with the sauces. It was very hard work. They were kind, the Major and Madam, but you had to work for your money there.

I had different work to do different days. On Wednesdays I had to scrub the hall floor. I thought it was a mile long. It didn't have no paint, polish, or nothing on it. Still, I had to

scrub that hall down, and I had to help in the kitchen as well.
I'd be in the kitchen all the time to help make the staff lunch
at three, the staff tea at five, and dinner for the house. The
Major and Madam used to have their dinners at eight o'clock
at night, after lunch and tea. I'd have to wait to wash up and
clean up all and put everything back in its place. I could be
in bed at half ten if I had me work done early, but if they
had visitors—a big party—I would't get to bed till half eleven
at night. Imagine the long hours, Sharon, and only a pound
a month. Later, they rose me wages to thirty shillings.

While I was there we had three cooks, a Scotch one and
two English ones. The first little cook was lovely. She was
from London and she was ever so tiny and real smart and
always jolly. She'd say, "You bleeding Irish!" But she'd help
me out everyway she could. I got real fond of this cook, but
she left and on comes a Scotch one. She was a villain. She
was as big as the table altogether. She was that fat, it'd take
her an hour to walk into the kitchen. She was nice at first,
and didn't I think she was like the English cook. But she
used to keep me all the time on me feet. She'd keep at me,
"Give me a pan. Give me that . . ." When I'd only go to sit
down in a chair, she'd give me another job to do and
another job. Me feet swelled and then didn't one of me legs
swell and I was sent to bed. Back out of bed, and still she
kept me on me feet.

One time she sent me on a message to the village. I
didn't want to go because I was afraid I'd miss me tea. It was
the cook's job to have a different cake every night for the
staff's tea, and I loved the cake. She knew it was tea time
and still she sent me down to Gretton. The village wasn't far
but when I got back, the tea was over and she'd left me
none of the cake. I said, "I got no cake from the tea." But
she passed no heed, just got up and walked away.

The next morning, I went to the pantry where Willie
would be cleaning the silver to get him to read the cook's
note, but he wasn't there. What am I going to do, I said to

meself. But I done the best I could on me own; I put out
kippers, eggs for scrambling, and laid the table. When the
cook came down, she said, "You Irish sod! You forgot one
thing."

"What was it? What was it!" I roared.

"You forgot the cream, the milk, for the scrambled eggs.
What way do you scramble your eggs in Ireland?" she said.
The next thing she hits me an awful slap and she caught me
be the hair and she pult me hair. I hated anyone to pull me
hair, Sharon. But she thought because I was soft, because I
used to cry with everything she'd say to me, that I wouldn't
tell. So she caught me be the hair and was going to thump
me for nothing. But I up with the pan and gave it to her
right across the side of the head. I just spinned around like
a top and gave it to her. Down she went in on top of the
range and her hands were nearly burned off.

Willie came along then. He was wanting something for
the dining hall and he looked at me and he looked at the
cook, "What happened? Did she take a heart attack?"

"No," said I. "I hit her a belt with the pan. I couldn't put
up with her and I'm giving in me notice." Willie left
down his tray and ran and brought in the mistress. In
she comes and the Major with his silver walking stick.

"What happened, Ann?" she said. But I wouldn't tell her.

"I want to get home," says I. "I want to get out of this kip."

"What do you mean? What do you mean, Ann?" she said.
She was annoyed with me then.

"I hate the English. I want to go home to Ireland," I said.

"Oh, Madam!" said the Major. "The Irish again. Madam,
didn't I tell you not to bring the Irish here."

"I'm Irish too. Leave Ann alone. Ann is a good girl,"
Madam said. I came back to meself then.

"Excuse me," says I. I thought to apologize to the Major
but he wouldn't look at me. "It's the Scotch I hate, not the
English," I said and started crying. I didn't know who I hated.

"What happened, Ann?" Madam Evans said.

"Madam," said I. (You couldn't call her "missus.")

"Madam," said I, "she was bullying me, telling me she could fight and all and I was afraid her." I *was* afraid of her, too. It was with the fear I hit her. "She was thumping me around and beating me around." Well, me jaw was red and me hair was messed up. "And Madam," I said, "I'm very sorry, but she got on me nerves."

"You'll have to be treated with your nerves," Madam said. "What did it all happen over?"

"It happened over the milk. I forgot the milk," I said. "She hit me a slap and caught me be the hair. I can't bear anyone doing that and I was afraid of her. She'd have been killing me. I had to take the pan to save meself."

I thought I was going to get the sack. And the shame, after Captain Grant, the Major and all sending me father to the Army and me father fighting for England, and for me to go from Ireland and make a show of him, his daughter—the sweep's daughter. But they didn't sack me. They liked me. They warned both me and the cook.

But what did I do to the cook? She was making cakes one day, and I was watching how to make them. And when she went out with the housemaid—a girl from the village— didn't I get every sort of fruit and wash it. But I didn't know how to weigh them; you have to be able to read to make a nice cake. But I mixed it all together anyway and made a lovely lookin' cake. Then it came to the icing. Says I, "Willie, brother, will you help me?"

"What do you want?" he said.

"I want you to help me do the icing," I said.

"Sure, aren't you with the cook long enough?" he said.

"But," said I, "I can't do it."

"All right, I'll do the icing then," he said. "What do you want this cake for?"

"I want this for the staff," I said. So he did the icing and he told me,

"Let it set."

"Right!" says I.

But hadn't I put a half pound of salt into the cake, and didn't I move the good cake, the one the cook had made, and put it into the staff. And I sent the salty cake into the Major.

The cook got the sack, no excuse. She told the Madam it wasn't her, but no. Poor Madam Evans said, "You're blaming that little Irish girl just because she comes from Ireland. I'm giving you a month's notice."

"I'm getting out of here before the month," she said.

"Well," said the Madam, "you won't get any reference. I won't give you a reference."

"I want nothing to do with the Irish," said the old cook. And away with her.

"Thanks be to Jesus," I said.

They got another cook then. She was lovely and I worked on real happy. And the Major got fond of me again. One day he asked me, "Ann, did you play that trick on the Scottish cook?"

"Oh, no," says I. "No sir!" Whenever the Madam or the Major came, you had to stand. You didn't have to salute them, but you had to stand up and I always used to say "sir" to the Major. "Oh, no sir," says I. "I did not." God forgive me, I was telling a lie. "No," says I, "but do you know what that cook done?"

"What did she do?" he said.

"She was going to poison me with the salt but the cake accidently went in to you. Now," says I, "wasn't she doing the dirt to the Irish?"

"Oh, I don't blame you," says he and he tapped me on the head. I loved the Major then. He was a lovely old Major.

Oh, I loved that place. The staff was good; it was like a family. We had our own dining hall, and the cook would sit at the top of the table. She was the head over us. The butler would sit next to her and the head housemaid on the other side.

This old housemaid was there for years. She was from

Wales. She used to do all the linen, sewing and all like this. She had an under housemaid and she'd tell her what to do and she'd go round to see what was right or wrong. Well, one day this old housemaid came into the dining hall and she took up her chair and banged it down. And then she took up her knife and fork and banged them agin the table. And when the cook stood up, the very minute she did, the housemaid got up and sat in the cook's place. We couldn't get her out of the cook's chair. But the cook pointed at us to say nothing. She knew that the poor woman's mind was going. And she was ever so nice, a clean person, lovely when she was all right. The next thing, didn't they take her away and she went to the mental.

The other housemaid wasn't very strong, so Madam herself came back and asked the cook her permission for me to go upstairs. The Madam couldn't say, "Ann will have to go upstairs, we're short of staff." She had to come in and ask the cook if she'd let me work as housemaid, and promise that they'd get her another girl. Well, the cook was willing enough, so Madam took me as housemaid and they rose me pay ten shillings more.

I was never lonesome because I loved me job. The Madam was very kind, even though she was a Protestant, and so was the Major. On a Saturday night she might say, "Ann, are you and William going to Mass in the morning?" She wouldn't tell us to go; she left it to ourselves. "If you're going to Mass," she'd tell me, "you'd better ask the cook." Or she might want me to do something before I'd go and she'd leave me an order to do it. I'd get two hours off of a Sunday and every second Sunday off. I used to love to get off for Mass in Corby. It was five miles away and there was an awful lot of Irish and Scots working there and an awful lot of factories. It was a great place.

I used to get a half day of a Wednesday off too. And after tea I'd get out. The tea hour would be over at four o'clock and I'd go round the village then walking round or across through the land. The village people'd say, "Here's mad Ann coming. Mad Ann's coming." Because I was Irish and I used to tell them off. But they liked me. The Major kept four bikes in the sheds for the staff, for any of us that wanted one to go out in the country for a spin on a Sunday or our half-days. The countryside was beautiful. There were viaducts just a quarter of a mile below Gretton, all little bridges for the trains to come over. And the village was pure beautiful.

In the winter the Major and Madam would go hunting for three weeks to Ireland or Scotland. They'd take their horses and dogs and go. The staff would love to get them gone. We had nothing to do then, just only keep the house nice. We'd have the house spotless, then we'd sit down and have a good time. I used to go up into the attic and look at all the toys and dolls and the rocking horse. And when they come back, the Major would bring rabbit, pheasants, hares, wild duck, geese, and deer. Whatever he had for the dining hall, he shared with us. It was great.

The Major had three daughters—Miss Shiela, Miss Jackie, and Miss Bunty. They had funny names. Miss Shiela was very motherly and sensible. She was thirty and dark haired. Miss Jackie was next. You'd never hardly see her wearing a skirt, she always wore trousers—the wide pants—riding boots, and the whip. She was a lovely looking girl, real blonde. Miss Bunty was the youngest. She was brown haired. They played tennis a lot and they loved their horses.

"Only one of them three girls got married, Sharon," Nan said, pausing for a moment's reflection. She pulled a stick out of the fire and lit a cigarette, then continued. "And the Major never had a son; that was the biggest mistake."

ONE TIME the Major gave me four dozen bantam hens. They were Miss Bunty's, only I looked after them. They were lovely. But what happened? Didn't I meet in with a boyfriend, and me and Tommie got too much of involved. He got in love with me, but I wasn't in love with him. It came Christmas and the bantams was growing grand and laying eggs. But this day Tommie said, "I'll take you to a dance, Ann."

"Right, Tommie," I said. And we went in to the dance. It was all old-time waltzing, fox trots, one-step two-step, scissors—all the old dances. I'm still good at them, too. Well, that time the dances used to be over at twelve. That night I was so tired, I forgot about me bantams—the dancing was in me head.

The next morning I got up and I had to do all me work. And when I was done, didn't I fall asleep. The cook was a real mother and at dinner she said, "Ann, you should go to bed early tonight." So I forgot all about me bantams.

It was cold that night and when I wakened up, I remembered and went out to look at the bantams, but they were all dead—only one. The frost killed them.

I couldn't tell the Major, so I went to Madam. Madam was like me mother, poor Mrs. Evans. "Madam," I said.

"What happened, Ann?" she said. "Tell me what happened." First I told her about Tommie. "You're in love with him?" said she.

"No," said I. "I'm not in love with him, but he's in love with me." She told me about the facts of life and all then. She told me when you go with boys never let them put their hand above your knees. And never let them maul you around. And don't be letting them kiss you too much: keep your lips closed. And even you love them, don't let them know it. Be friendly to them. All this sort of thing. She was a lady.

"But, Madam," I said. Then I told her about the bantams. "How will you explain to the Major?" I said. "The Major bought them for Miss Bunty for a present." I started sobbing then over the bantams.

"Don't cry, Ann," said the Madam.

Later the Major came down. "Don't worry, Ann," he said. "I'm going to buy you a lovely present." It was a surprise. I got a lovely pair of flat shoes with buckles—it was the Madam that got them—and a white blouse with all tucks and a collar, and a green costume with one pleat in front and one pleat behind. It was tight fitting and real green.

"Now," said the Madam. "The Major wants to see you Sunday dressed in that." Well, I was eleven stone [143 lbs.] then and had real long red hair and terrible freckles. I tied me hair at the neck and it was hanging down me back all in curls. They took a photo of me. "How are you, Ann?" asked the Major when he saw me.

"Oh, thank you, Sir. It's beautiful. Do you know what I love so much?" I said.

"What do you love so much?" he said. I don't know whether I insulted the Major or not then. He was English but I forgot.

"Oh," said I, "I love it because it's green. Isn't it a lovely green colour."

The Madam put her eyes on me for mentioning it. "Oh," she said, "that's why the Major bought it for you."

"Well," he said, "I'm proud of you." And he clamped me on the back. "I love an Irish lady too."

Regrettably for Nan, her days at Gretton House were coming to an end. She was forewarned of this late one night when she heard something outside the small dormer window of her attic bedroom.

ONE NIGHT I couldn't sleep and I got up and went to the window. I heard a cry and the cry was very lonely and bitter. So I looked at the housemaid and I said, "Do you hear anything? Come to the window. I heard a cry."

"You're mad," she said. "All you Irish is mad." You know the way the English think, Sharon. "You must be tired," she said. "You over done yourself with work today."

"Oh, all right," I said. "You go back to sleep." I didn't like to disturb her. But then, didn't she get nervous.

"I can't sleep either," she said and she put on her slippers and went and knocked at Willie's door.

"What's wrong?"

"Do you hear anything?"

"I did," he said. "I thought I heard a cry."

"I'm after hearing it terrible," I said.

"There's somebody dead belonging to us," Willie said. "It's the banshee."

Whenever there'd be anyone dying belonging to the Travellers, they'd hear the banshee. Not every Traveller, the banshee only follows the real Irish names—O'Connors, O'Donohoes—all the people with so many Os to their name. The country people in Ireland believe this, too, but they tell you, you won't hear it in England or across water. But that's a lie. I heard it in England.

"Don't tell me that," I said to Willie. "Don't tell me that when you're going home tomorrow. Don't scare me while you'll be gone." And I started to worry about me mother, because of the banshee crying.

"I'll write," he said. "I'll let you know straight away. Don't worry, Nan. If there's anything wrong, you can come straight over."

Willie went on the next day. He had to go home to do his training in the Irish Army. The Major was very good and let him go home. I used to have to stay and work away. When he got home, he sent a telegram straight to the Major. Me granny—me mother's mother, the Lord have mercy on her—was dying. Well, I wasn't much worried then. I was sorry about me grandmother, but I was glad that me mother was safe.

—————————————

A few months later, however, Nan's mother did become ill and entered Longford hospital. Nan was sent for to help her father care for the younger children.

COMING HOME on that train, Sharon, I cried. I didn't want to go. Me brother went with me. I cried meself sick till I got there. But I was the only one that could help. Chrissie was at home but she wasn't much good to help. And the older girls, that was well grown up and educated, had gone off to work or else got married and went off. So I had to go back. Me mother was bad. I don't know what happened to her but she was in hospital when I went home.

Leaving Gretton House in early 1939 was difficult for Nan. Her brush with "the quality" even as a domestic, always seemed to her to have been her one true brush with luck. "Wasn't it a big miss I didn't stay in England, Sharon," she often said to me when depressed. "I had me chance that time. I wish to God I never left England." And when her sons and daughters made her angry, Nan would yell, "I may look thick and ignorant now but I worked with first-class people." But they'd invariably remind her, "But you were a second-class person. You were working for them." Travellers have few illusions and maintain few pretenses.

In England the Evans' family fortunes also changed. War was declared on the third of September 1939. Major Evans formed a local defense volunteers chapter the following year. But in 1943 he sold Gretton House to Stewarts and Lloyd's, the Corby-based steelworks, which in turn leased it to the army. Central heating was installed and it was used as a transit hospital during the remainder of the war. After the war, the house returned to the steel mill and served as a rehabilitation center for injured steelworkers until 1980 when economic recession necessitated its sale once more.

By then only two of the Evanses were still living: Miss Bunty, married and in England; and Miss Jackie, single and living in Ireland in Rathconrath House, the Grants' old residence. She had moved there in the early 1970s with her elderly mother, Madam Evans, who had retained a partial interest in the house.

When I visited the house, I had not expected to meet Miss Jackie. I didn't even know she lived there. I was merely visiting the places Nan had lived and traveled. But when she came to the door, I knew.

Although in her mid-sixties, she was still wearing riding pants and boots. And I had arrived inopportunely in the middle of the Cheltenham races. She led me into the cramped and cluttered kitchen where she was fixing a bowl of meat and meal for her dogs on a two-ring gas burner sitting on a marble-topped dresser. A television was balanced on a chair a few feet away, horses running. An aged black dog named Sweep lay on an old coat in the corner snoring loudly, and while we watched, another dog listed across the room. Miss Jackie was lively and coolly courteous. It amused her that someone should think it important to write the story of a tinker's life. But Americans were always doing strange things— she as much as said so.

She remembered little of Nan, much more of "William." As a combination butler and parlormaid, he had had more direct contact with the family. She described him as handsome and polite, except once when he had snapped at her while her parents were away and he was busy washing windows. But he had gone to the Madam when she had returned and apologized for having been "very rude to Miss Jackie."

He lived in a house in London now, was married and had two children. He had made a modest success of his life. It was apparent that Miss Jackie approved far more of William than of Nan who had remained a Traveller. To Miss Jackie, it was as if Nan had purposely and foolishly chosen to do so. Or perhaps she was just unconcerned. After all, Nan had only been a kitchen maid.

I V

The Unwilling Wife

It was on the road the summer of 1939—the hottest and driest for fifteen years—that Nan met Jim Browne. He was twenty-nine and more than ripe for matrimony; unmarried men have little status among Travellers for whom the family is everything and even the word "friend" means a relative.[16] At nineteen, Nan was no longer a girl either. She was an attractive, if slightly plump, young woman.

"That summer I was ashamed of meself, Sharon," Nan said to me one morning. We were sitting outside her trailer. The first hint of autumn was in the air, and the backs of my hands were cold. Nan had just stoked the fire and was now swirling boiling water in a battered aluminum pot. She tossed it out, then dug three heaping spoonfuls of tea out a narrow rectangular package, filled the kettle with fresh water, replaced the lid, and manipulated some burning boards to create a flat resting spot. I sat on an overturned crate—the car seat had disappeared—and warmed my hands, while Nan squatted next to the brewing tea.

ME ARMS was stout and me two legs used to brush agin one another when I'd go to walk. It was all the pieces of cake the cook used to give me. And I was terrible red; I had a terrible sunburn and freckles all over. That's when I met Browne.

Me and Chrissie used to go to the pictures in Mullingar—
it was only four pence to get in—and we met Jim Browne
there. We already knew him and he knew us on account of
our families travelling and meeting. His parents weren't real
Travellers, though. His mother belonged to the town of
Granard, and his father was from a farming family in the
county Westmeath. But when his father came back from the
war, the 1914 War, he started to drink—a person's never the
same after war—and in the end, he couldn't pay for his
house, even though houses were only cheap at the time. He
started his family on the road then. Three of the sons stayed
on the road.

Well, Jim started coming up to see me then. He used to
cycle to where we was camped. He kept going and coming
back, going and coming back, different days and different
hours in the day. He'd never keep away. Wherever my father
would travel, Jim'd follow on the bike. And he was real
sneaky; he'd sit down chatting to me father and pay no heed
to me. Whenever I seen him coming, I'd sneak away down
the road or run in through the fields. I never liked any of
the Brownes much. They thought they were too good for
everyone and that the rest of the Travelling People was only
dirt. They always stayed out on their own and held their
nose up.

But Nan was also interested in someone else—Brendan, a
laborer's son from Ballynacargy. It was a harmless flirtation,
but Nan's father did not approve of Brendan's lazy ways and
fondness for clothes and had threatened him once with a
chimney scrapper: "If I ever catch you around me daughter
or me fire again, I'm going to kill you." So Brendan kept
away, waiting out of sight down the road. There he and Nan
made daisy chains, talked, and joked, often at Jim's expense.

"BROWNE'S a lovely gentleman," me father said to me one day. "A fine man. He's quiet and respectable. You should marry Brown."

"No! No marriage!" I roared and I run off through the fields.

But in the end, me father said, "You're going to marry Browne, now. He's a nice fellow and he's followed us all over the country." I didn't have any choice.

"I'll marry him," I said, "but I don't like him. I hate him. And the very minute I marry him, I'm never going to live with him."

And with that, a matched marriage was made.[17]

Nan wed Jim Browne in Mullingar on the July 21, 1939, with two other Travellers, John Keenan and Annie Byrne, as witnesses. But unlike most newlyweds who remained in the same county as their parents, Nan and Jim moved to Dublin. There they camped in Terenure on the southern edge of the city, at a spot frequented by Travellers. Nan walked from door to door peddling scrubbing brushes, shoe polish, needles and thread, while Jim played the accordion and passed his hat in pubs. He was nice to Nan, but living with him was a strangely isolating experience and Nan was unhappy.

"I don't think Jim ever knew his own mind," Nan tried to explain.

HE DIDN'T speak much. I was often there with him all day—I'd be washing or baking or something—and he wouldn't give me three words. He'd play: he'd take up the accordion and play. Or else he'd walk down the road look-ing after his ponies. And if he seen other Travelling People coming, he'd get into the field or go on up the road. He wouldn't stand to speak to them. He was a fella that only loved to be on his own. I never really knew him; I don't think he knew himself. He was nice enough, fair play to him. He was nice to me first, but I never did care about him. I didn't want him; he was too quiet. He never loved me either. He only wanted a wife; he was getting old.

Nan left Jim twice in the first year, something young Travelling brides often did. The first time, she caught a train to Mullingar and stayed a few days with friends. The second time, in April 1940, she simply walked away. She had been sitting in a pub in the Combe, an old part of the city, with Jim and her aunt and uncle—the same aunt and uncle she had visited while working in Dun Laoghaire. They were talking and on the surface, everything seemed fine. Nan put down her glass of Guinness and got up from the booth to walk to the ladies room. She walked to Kilcock instead, straight out the back door of the pub and down the road to Kilcock, ten miles away. Her feet were swollen by the time she got there. She met the Hands, a Travelling family she knew, and spent the night. The next morning she set out for Mullingar, resting her bruised feet and psyche overnight in the county home, a hostel for the homeless. The following day she reached her parents' house in Edgeworthstown.

I STAYED about three months with me father and mother. They loved to have me there, but that time there was no such thing as the assistance—the family allowance—and I wouldn't beg around Edgeworthstown, not if I was to be kilt. And then me father never forgiven himself over me marriage. Me mother blamed him too and they were always fighting over it.

Nan would have stayed longer, despite the arguments and financial strain, but by now she was obviously pregnant. Her father sent a letter to Jim, who was staying with his mother in the nearby village of Moate, and Jim dutifully fetched her. They returned to Dublin, and in November young James was born.

I REMEMBER having me first baby, Sharon. I took pains and I thought I was getting bad, and Jim was so nervous that he took me straight into Hollis Street hospital. I was there for a night and there was no sign of the baby, and the doctors said I had about three weeks to go. So we came home. We were staying in a tent on Terenure Lane. But I was only back two weeks when I got bad again. This time Jim took me to the old Coombe hospital. I had no bother having little James. I thought it was going to be worse, but it wasn't all that bad even though he was a very big child. He was near ten pound born. And it's a funny thing, after having James I begin to like Jim in a sort of way.

Nan and Jim apparently did get along well for quite a while after James's birth. They camped on the roadside in Dublin until spring and then travelled west by horse and cart to Galway where sturdy, dark-legged Connemara ponies ran wild through the rocky, windswept mountains and blanket bogs. It was a "backward" place where farmers rarely saw a dealer. Jim and his brother Michael decided to fill the void, paying farmers £5 a piece for one- and two-year-old foals. It took a full day for them to catch the ponies, but it was worth the effort since they fetched a good price in the east. When they had a herd assembled, they drove them back to Dublin where they were sold to Travellers and to settled horse dealers at the Smithfield fair.

The Brownes crisscrossed the country for almost two years. Nan had a daughter named Eileen. But as more and more Travellers entered the trade, farmers began to ask for more money. And as the trips became less and less profitable, Jim "quit the ponies" and returned to Dublin.

Instead of staying on the roadside, they moved in temporarily with Jim's mother who now lived in a tiny flat on Meath Street in the heart of the "Liberties"—Dublin's oldest neighborhood. It was a bustling place, filled with fruit and vegetable dealers, cheap clothing stores, and shoppers haggling amid the shrill song of women street vendors. Jim returned to "musicianing," riding his bicycle from town to town in the Midlands and playing his accordian at factory gates, pubs, and fairs. He slept in county homes and cheap lodging houses, mixing more with tramps than other Travelling People. Nan stayed in Dublin with James and Eileen, and soon she was expecting again.

I WENT into the old Coombe again, and that's where I had Angela, me second little daughter. That time in Ireland, you had to stay eight days in hospital after your baby. They wouldn't let you out before. And you had to have your husband collect you. Well, I waited the eight days Sharon and I didn't see Browne. It came the ninth day and no still sign of him. I began to worry then, because if you weren't a married woman, they sent you to a home—a convent—to work until they got your child adopted out. There was a place like that in Castlepollard, near Mullingar, for unfortunate girls. Well, the nurses came to enquire where me husband was. They thought I wasn't married. So I told them, "Ring up Mullingar. That's where I was married." But they didn't. Finally, the guards went round the camps to find out if I had anybody, and the next thing, Browne's sister came to see me.

"I came to take you out," she said.

"Where is he?" I said.

"He's gone to the country."

I believed her, but when I came out, I heard a different

story. He was gone off with another woman. The shock of it, with a baby only nine days old, near killed me. That's what broke me and him up. I was on me own then with three small children and no home to go to.

This is the version of their separation that Nan first told me, and most of it did happen. Yet as she revealed in later conversations she had left Jim on several occasions. Just six months before Angela's birth, she had gone to Mullingar, this time to visit her brother Pat who had been hit by a train and had a leg amputated. She and little Eileen stayed two weeks instead of the couple days she had promised, and when Jim did not see her returning, he placed young James in institutional care. After that, Nan "couldn't bear to live with him. He had no nature, no love for wife or child." So she left.

Too ashamed to return to her parents and unwelcome at Jim's mother's, she found a room on Patrick Street across from St. Patrick's Cathedral and the park. It cost a shilling and six pence a night for little more than a bed. When Nan went into hospital to have Angela five months later, Jim was camped on Red Cow Lane in Terenure, about three miles away, but he never came to collect her. During the intervening months, he had indeed taken up with another woman.

A year of real hardship for Nan then began. Living in a rented room in Engine Alley, she had even less security than a Traveller on the road. She had to pay for her room each day, knowing that if anyone the landlord liked better came along, she would lose it. It was a rough part of the city, a place where prostitutes flourished and any single woman was suspect.

One evening Nan returned home with Eileen and Angela and struggled up the dimly-lit stairs. The small window over the front door was so grimy, it was always dark in the hallway no matter what time of day. She gripped Angela in one arm and clutched her groceries and Eileen's hand with the other.

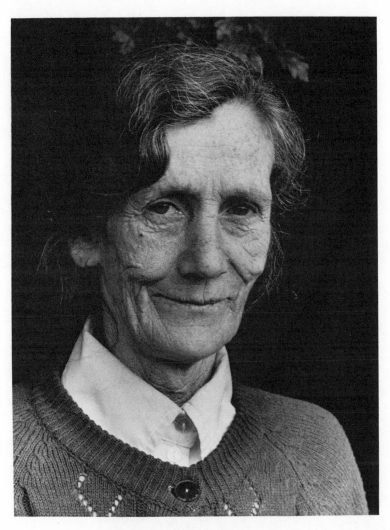

Nan Donohoe in 1972. *(George Gmelch)*

ABOVE. Granard, CO. Longford—Nan's birthplace—in the early part of this century. *(Lawrence Collection, National Library of Ireland)*
LEFT. A Travelling woman with two of her daughters "calling" at farmhouses in CO. Longford in the early 1930s. *(Padraig MacGreine)*

ABOVE. Gretton House in Gretton, Northamptonshire, where Nan worked as a kitchen maid in the mid-1930s. *(George Gmelch)*

BELOW. A Travelling couple makes a meal on the side of the road in the early 1940s. Many Travellers kept a goat for milk. *(Father Browne Collection, Dublin)*

ABOVE. The Liberties of Dublin in the early 1900s. Nan stayed here in the 1940s, but the basic appearance of the area was much as it looks here. *(Lawrence Collection, National Library of Ireland)*
LEFT. Mick Donohoe poses with his pony at Holylands on the outskirts of Dublin in 1972. *(George Gmelch)*
RIGHT. Michael Donohoe *(foreground)* and Anthony Maugham give the author's mare a rest on a journey to Blessington, co. Wicklow in 1972. *(George Gmelch)*

ABOVE. A Traveller fashions tinware on the roadside near Galway City in 1972. A jack-of-all-trades, he also keeps a bundle of chimney sweeping rods and brushes tied to his bicycle. *(George Gmelch)*
BELOW. Travelling children listen to their mother under the exposed ribs of a bender tent in co. Mayo in 1978. *(George Gmelch)*

Nan had a key to her room, but this night the door pushed open easily. "What the fuckin' Jesus," said a startled red-haired woman lying in Nan's bed. Nan jerked the door shut, and she and little Eileen and Angela slept on the first-floor landing that night. The next day, she was lucky enough to find a room in nearby Meath Street. But still, life was far from easy.

I DIDN'T know what to do, Sharon. I couldn't go home to me mother because of what the neighbors would think and of what the Travelling People would think too. I was ashamed to go home. And I couldn't get a job with the kids. I used to go to the convents to get bread and milk. There was no welfare like today to help you out. There was only the "cruelty," and if you went and complained or said you had no way to keep yourself, the kids was taken from you. So I'd go along the bus queues. That time they'd be about a mile in length, because there wasn't so many buses as now. I'd go along with Angela and Eileen and ask all the people in the queue for help, but I had to hide from the guards. I was scared to death of the guards—I couldn't do jail, not with the kids—and if I only seen one of them, I'd tremble.

If I got any few pence at all, I'd go back to me room and pay me rent. I often starved meself. Many a time I went hungry to buy milk and food for the kids. And on a wet day if I hadn't enough money, I'd have to get somebody to mind them—to baby-sit—and go out on me own. Women'd baby-sit for two shillings a week because two shillings was a lot at that time.

I used to be scared and I felt very down and out. I was a very bad beggar. I was bad because I wasn't brought up to the begging, I was used to work. Me father made us all go out and work. Well, if you're used to working, and then you have to go ask anything or anybody, you'd rather starve. I tried for a job a couple of times. I went to the Mater Hospital; I tried a couple of hospitals, but I could get no job. So I had to beg, just enough to see that the children wasn't hungry.

Them times people in Ireland was very comical. They thought if your marriage was broke up, that you were to live on by yourself. They thought that you should find a job. But I hadn't enough of education to get around on me own. Oh, I could have gettin' a job with a farmer—you wouldn't need an education for that—but you'd be slaved to death for a couple of bob a week. I'd rather go on and tramp the roads whatever was to happen to me. Well, in the end I could only just bear to live on me own.

During this time, Nan met Mick Donohoe—a second cousin. He was thirty years old, a widower with four young sons who were being cared for by his mother who lived near Nan on Church Lane. Nan met him one day while visiting her aunt, and soon Mick was taking Nan to the cinema and to the Iveagh market to buy shoes. He was dark haired, handsome, and fun. He also provided protection in the city. "City boys, when they'd hear a country voice, would be after you thinking you were a prostitute," Nan explained. They saw each other fairly often over the next six months; Mick all the while telling Nan she was a fool to keep on the way she was. "You'd be better off if you got out of this country," he said. "Go to England or the North. The North is great."

Nan resisted at first, but gradually Mick won her over. The North did offer a new beginning, and, as with so many decisions in her life, Nan felt compelled to go. Her life in Dublin was unbearable; the North was a place to run and hide.

ME NERVES was gone. And Mick was all the time telling me about the North and saying, "You're a fool to stay here." So I said to meself, I'll try it and even if I don't like it, I might get a job. It wasn't to go with Mick that I went. I just had to get away. So I give Eileen to me sister Mary to look after and Angela to me mother and me sister Eileen who was living at home. I had to hand them up; I couldn't keep them on me own.

The exact story of the circumstances under which Nan gave her children up and with what understanding her sisters took them has been lost in the mists of time and guilt. But not long after Nan left for the North with Mick, both children were returned to Jim Browne. Nan's angry mother and reluctant sisters found him camping near the "Seven Lock Canal" in Palmerstown. He in turn gave three-year-old Eileen to his mother to raise and sent infant Angela to an orphanage in Cork. As Nan said simply, "That was the end of the kids, and the starting of me and Mick. Wasn't my life terrible sad."

V

Travelling in the North

It was wartime. Ireland remained neutral, but thousands of foreign troops, mainly Americans, were based in Northern Ireland which became the main training center for Allied troops.[18] Belfast's shipyards and factories pulsed with activity; there were military contracts to fill and merchant ships to maintain.[19] Farmers worked from dawn to dusk, plowing up pasturage to plant wheat under compulsory tillage orders. It seemed the place to go.

So in the autumn of 1943, Nan and Mick took the train from Dublin to Belfast. Once there, they made their way to Little George Street. Nan's eldest sister, Lizzie, with whom she had lived as a child, had left Ballymahon and moved to the North. With her second husband, Joe, an ex-sergeant in the Free State Army, she now ran a second-hand shop, with "digs" for dockers and other laboring men above.

Lizzie took them in, but they stayed in separate rooms since, as Nan described it, "We never lived as man and wife then." After a few days, Mick rented a room in another lodging house and began walking from door to door offering to mend old pots and pans. He carried his tinsmithing tools in a "budget" on his back and found plenty of work. New metal wares, as well as the money to buy them, were scarce and his skills were needed. Nevertheless, Mick made just enough money to support himself and he began to look for wage work. Two weeks later, he found a job in the vast Harland and Wolff shipyards, replacing one of the thousands of Irish workers from both North and South who had joined the military or gone to England to work.

"Mick'd come back at night, Sharon, and sit with us," Nan began. We were alone in her trailer; everyone had gone off for the day, including the children. It was about eleven and Nan was just sitting down with a cup of tea. I took the mug she offered me, pushed aside a pile of laundry, and sat down on the edge of the fold-out bed.

THEN HE'D go out for a drink. I didn't drink that time, so I'd stay in Lizzie's house. In the day, I'd look after things in the shop while she'd go off to auctions, buying gold rings, old furniture, anything she could. At first, me brother-in-law Joe was all right. But he had an old Dublin woman working around the place that he used to pay and he thought a lot about her. He already had the one woman, so he didn't need me. I don't think he wanted me to be with me sister anyways. I was there a few months—I stayed the winter, then I left. Mick quit his work on the docks because he thought they'd found out he was a Catholic. If you were a Catholic then, you got no chance on the docks.

We started off travelling. We just made off. We had nothing—no pony, no nothing. Me sister gave me a basket when I was going and a few pounds, and I bought some stuff to sell: combs, plates, cups, needles, thread, scissors, anything that would suit. I bought it in the wholesale shops. You had to buy a dozen of everything to get them half price, but you could make a good few bob selling. We went on travelling then. We walked and we lay out.

Some nights a farm might have a big shed, and we'd lay in it. But it wasn't every night that we'd get one of them. Most nights we lay under hedges on the side of the road. And me feet used to be sore. We often walked thirteen, fourteen mile a day. Mick used to fix pots and pans and make tins. It was hard to get tin during the war; you had to have permits or know somebody that knew you. But Mick, thank God, was lucky. I sold my things and I started reading fortunes—reading cards. I told people all the lies I could, just to get the few bob. I used to be trembling but still I managed. That's how we started out. We didn't settle down no more then.

When we left Belfast, we lived as man and wife. We were lying out here and there together. We walked for weeks and lay out because there was nobody to take us in. There was one little town in the North, Lurgan. The Travelling People put the name "Ha'penny Lurgan" on it because any charity you'd get there, it'd be only a ha'penny. There was digs there for Travelling People. It was a very big house, like a lodging house. Single men was put on their own and single women. There might be four beds in one room. The married couples had other rooms.

"That time you had to have your identity papers—who you were and all. You had to have a pass, like a little passport with your photo in it. Mick had one because he'd been in and out through the North before. But I had nar a one. But the lady of the lodging house knew Mick, "Ah, you're back."

"Yeah," he said, "me wife's with me now."

"Oh, that's grand," she said and she shook hands with me. She was ever so nice and it was a lovely place, clean and everything. "Now, Mick," says she, "where's her passport?" I had none.

"Ah," said he, "I'm only after bringing her in. I'll have to bring her to get one."

"Oh, no," she said, "I can't keep her." But she kept us anyway for two nights. I couldn't show me nose out the door. I couldn't even go into the dining hall to eat. She hid me in her own room. Oh, I was freckened. We went on then and didn't get any more digs. We had to stay out, in cold weather and all.

We didn't know much about the North, and we came to a place that was nothing only land, miles and miles and not a house. We started walking over this gap and we kept going and going and there was nothing. We walked and we kept walking. I said to Mick, "This is a funny part of the country. Is all the North like this? There's not a house."

"This is gap, something like the Curragh," he said, "there's no houses for miles." But he thought it'd only be a couple of miles.

It took us all day and it was coming night. We were jaded and me feet hurt. I had to take off me shoes and walk in me bare feet. And we were starving with the hunger. We had some money but we had nothing with us, no way of making our tea. We thought we'd meet a shop or see a house and go in and ask them to make us some tea.

"Well," said I, "I'm weak." And I begin to cry with this long journey. Finally we seen some houses and we made on to them. I went to the door and I forgot meself, thinking I was up in me own part of the country. I knocked and said, "God save everybody in."

"Who's that?" a woman said. There was no answer back, "God save you," or anything like that. Well, I didn't pass no heed to it. A woman came to the door.

"God bless you, ma'am. We're half dead," I said. "We're after coming across miles of a place and me feet is killing me. I'll say three Hail Marys for you, ma'am, if you make us a cup of tea." This is the way you'd beg in the South. If you said a Hail Mary, they'd believe and give you anthing. The woman kept staring at me. Wasn't I in a Protestant part of the North, what they call the "real Orange."

"Your poor feet is in a bad way," she said.

"I'm ruined," I said.

"You mustn't be Travelling People," she said.

"We are Travelling People but we met with a bit of bad luck and anything we had, we got rid of it. And we left our people," I said, telling her the truth like about what did happen. "We run away down here to this part of the country. We had a bit of trouble with our own friends and we came down to this part of the country just to see could we get on," I said.

"Well," she said. "I pity the ways ye are. Is that your husband?"

"Yes."

"The Travelling People is very cheeky here," says she. "They don't go on the way you do."

"Ah," said I, "there's good and bad everywhere."

"Sit down," said she. "Call in your husband." And she put down big slices of bacon for ourselves and plenty of bread. She said to Mick, "Can you work?"

"I can," he said. And so he could. Mick always did work, doing tinsmithing or anything like that. He'd rather work than anything.

"Can you do farming work?" says she.

"I can do any work," said Mick, and he told her about where he used to work in Scotland and in England before we was married.

"Well," said she, "all right then. Wait now till me husband comes in and I might get something for you to do." She made us a feed and he came in.

"Have you no where to sleep?" he said. "Go out there to the barn tonight." We were glad to get lying, we were so tired.

The next morning they called us. And the farmer said to Mick, "If you want to stay here for a few weeks, there's a cow house down there." In the field there was a little barn. "It's all right. I'll get the boys to give it a sweep out. We'll put straw and blankets in there and it will do yourself and the missus. And will you do a bit of work for me? I'm short of hands. I need a man bad." Well, then Mick started to work for them. He helped them sow potatoes and weedin' and all different work. The farmer needed him.

The woman could call me up, and I'd help her with the

house. I'd clean up, wash, scrub the floors, tables, and she used to love to have me. She learned me how to milk and I watched her making cakes. I can make cakes now just like she done. And she learned me how to make butter—farmer's butter. She'd get down this little churn. It was made out of wood and was real brown on the outside. It was a beautiful little thing with little cog wheels and a handle out of it. She'd put in the milk and throw so many handfuls of salt into it and then throw boiling water in on top of that. It had to be boiling. And then she put the lid on with a little white cloth to keep it tidy. And then she'd go ahead churning, spinning the handle around. It took over two hours. Everyone would take a turn, until they'd get butter. They'd rise the lid and you'd see all the butter in little pieces coming to the top. She'd take it out and beat it. She had a big wooden bowl and two wooden spoons. Then she'd make it all into pounds in little glass shapes—diamond shapes, different shapes. That'd be for the shop and their own house. It was salt butter, real yellow.

Any buttermilk that would be left over, the farmers used to drink it. They weren't so fond of tea on warm summer days when they'd be making hay. The wife or daughter would bring down a big tin can of buttermilk instead. And if there was six men in the house, there'd always be six mugs in the kitchen. And they'd take them down and they'd drink a big three-quart can of buttermilk along with their dinner—plenty of cabbage, potatoes, and bacon. We ended up seven months with them. We saved a right lot of money. I wouldn't take no money off them, but they paid Mick. And they gave us everything free.

Nan and Mick took their savings and returned to Belfast for the winter, staying in a cheap lodging house. When spring came, they went to Walter Cunningham, a horse dealer with a reputation for being fair—"If he knew you were poor, he'd give you a good horse and he wouldn't rob you. But if you were rich, then he would"—and bought a small reddish-brown pony with a silver mane and four white feet. They named him Tom. They bought an inexpensive flat cart with rubber tires from another Traveller and then splurged on a new canvas tent cover which cost ten pounds, nearly as much as both pony and cart. They were now ready to travel in comfort.

They left Belfast, travelling west through Down and into counties Armagh and Tyrone. These were happy days or should have been. The weather was fine; warm air swirled around them. The green fields shimmered in the sunlight. The landscape, unencumbered by gray, seemed open and expansive. Crows, so ominous in the wet and cold, now sounded cheerful and free. Tom's hooves tapped out a pleasing rhythm on the dirt lanes which rose and fell gently, following the contours of the neatly cultivated hills. Mick held the reins lightly as they bounced along. They talked little and instead watched the birds flitting in and out of the hawthorn hedgerows.

Despite wartime rationing, Nan and Mick experienced no shortages. As Travellers, they were buffered from the full effects of the war by their own resilience and by the self-sufficiency and generosity of the farming community. Down was one of the most fertile counties in Ireland. Armagh was known as the "garden of Ulster," an area of apple and plum orchards and fields of strawberries, raspberries, and currants which flourished in the peaty soil. They camped by water whenever they could. It was convenient and "homely"—every chore seemed easier and every evening less lonely against the sound and movement of a river or stream.

Nan went out each morning to sell and beg at the farmhouses. Mick kept busy fishing, snaring rabbits, making tinware, and helping Nan with her chores. In the late afternoon, they met to sit by the fire and recount the day's events. And every now and then something unexpected would happen.

WE WERE camped one time in a beautiful place in the
county Tyrone. We were pult in on the side of the road outside a small little village near Dungannon. I can't think of
the name. This is the first time I ever seen American troops,
Sharon. We had our tent up and it was going on evening
time. It was a lovely camp, along a big river. But anyhow,
two big jeeps pult up and the Americans jumped down and
came in round the fire, real homely like. I got afraid for me
life. "Oh," I said. "What are they? Is there trouble?" And I
begin to tremble.

"Don't be getting nervous," said Mick. I was expecting a
baby that time. "Don't be getting nervous. It's Yanks. They're
harmless." They had their camp just down below us.

Well, one fella took out a box of chewing gum and
offered me some. I was delighted with it. I was chewing and
wouldn't part with it. So he gave it to me.

"Here," he said, "have more." When he spoke, I could
hardly understand him.

When they seen us so poor, they all took out money and
threw it to me. I was sitting down. Some of them threw me
American money and some of them threw me English
money. Then they got up in their jeeps and went on. But
that evening, one of the jeeps comes back and they left
down a box of food—a big bag of tea, sugar, jam (the big
old time pots, a crockery jar, that they used to have the marmalade in), and a heap of butter. They got it all out of their
canteen. And they left down this big box of food. Ah, it'd do
me and Mick for months. We were delighted with it.

We met more Travelling People and I told them about
the soldiers, how good they were. And the women said,
"You should beg all them soldiers, they're good. We had
nothing, but we're made up now. We're after buying new
covers." I was cursing meself then, because the women told
Mick. I said to meself, I wish to God they didn't tell him
because he'll want me to go in and beg them all. I started
begging them then, but I used to hate it. I never did like

begging. But we got a right few pound together. They were
very good-hearted, the Yanks. But then they left. They went
back. For months after, the Travelling women got it very
hard because they had to go out and look for the money
and they couldn't get it the way they had when the Yanks
was there.

These should have been good days for Nan. Mick was good
company. He was an observant person and had many stories
to tell of his experiences and travels in the South and of work
in Scotland. His confidence and good humor were reassuring. Yet Nan was often troubled. It was difficult to keep her
mind on the present, the past slipped too easily into view.
And from other Travellers she had learned some tragic news.
Her daughter Eileen had been killed in Dubin, crushed
between a lamp post and a cart loaded with timber while
playing in Engine Alley next to Molyneux Lane—an old
Huguenot street that still houses three draft horses in a stable
in the middle of a scrap metal yard. The horse had apparently
been startled by other children and backed up suddenly, pin-
ning Eileen.

MICK was kind to me that time, Sharon. He was very kind.
But no matter how good he was, I wasn't happy. I wasn't
happy at all. I knew I was living wrong—going off and going
round with Mick with me husband living in another place
and me kids gone. And then Eileen getting killed. . . . It was
a cross in front of me, and I had to go through it. Some days
I didn't care if I was dead.

I felt ashamed for me own people. Me father and me
mother was good people. All of me people were good living, and they didn't believe in what I done. I was scared to
see me family. I was worried that I could never face me
brothers or me mother and father again. This is what I'd be
thinking of all the time.

But it wasn't long before I did. We were camped in a little

village outside Portadown, when Mick bumped into me
brother John. They went in for a drink and Mick told him
all, how we were together and how I was pregnant. Well,
me brother didn't like it, and the two of them started fighting. They boxed out in the street—me brother was going to
kill Mick—and they got arrested over it. I run away to some
other Travelling People to hide there for a few days. But me
brother found me and came to speak to me. He asked me to
go back to me mother.

"No," I said, "I won't." John, the Lord have mercy on him,
was very kind, very forgiving. But I'd rather keep away from
all belonging to me. I did keep away then. I didn't go near
me family for years. I never went back home, only when me
mother got sick years after. I had to face me family then, but
they didn't say anything because I was too long away. I was
too far gone.

Mick and Nan continued traveling in the North after the
fight. Oddly, it seemed easier to enjoy the summer now that
her fate was more tightly intertwined with his; he had fought
for her and she had confronted her brother and decided never
to return home. Much of the worry and vulnerability disappeared, replaced by a resolve to live. Slowly, Nan made peace
with herself.

I USED to get up very early in the morning. I used to love
getting up. I couldn't sleep anyway, I'd get a terrible head-
ache. But Mick could sleep until nine or ten, or twelve if he
was let. I used to wash meself and walk down to the fields
with the winkers to catch Tom and let him out. We used to
sneak him into the fields at night unknownst to the farmers.
Tom was a real pet. Whoever reared him, it must have been
a woman because he used to run with excitement to get to
me. The horse was that delighted to see me going to the
fields that he'd made a run for me with his mouth open. He

used to scare me, rearing and pounding his feet but he never touched me. He was a pet of a horse.

And Tom was that clever. I used to take him out with me to sell. Mick was making tins at the time, and I was selling me own work out of a basket. And that time we used to collect scrap—copper, aluminia, brass. If the farmer had any, I'd give him something out of me basket for it. If I seen a piece of copper or a bit of aluminia, I'd give him a comb or a scrubbing brush, but what I'd be getting might be worth a couple of pounds. I used to collect the scrap for a month, then we'd take it back to the nearest town, Belfast or Newtownards. There'd always be a Jew man there to buy it. Well, between Mick's tins and the scrap, I used to have to bring the pony with me.

So I trained Tom. I'd go into the houses to sell or beg and Tom would come and wait by the gate. Even if I was a long way down the avenue, he'd wait. I'd shout, "Stand Tom, stand!" And I'd keep going in and out to the houses collecting and selling. I'd go as far as he could see me, maybe a quarter or a half a mile along a straight road and I'd just shout "Come on, Tom," and wave me hand. Tom would come galloping. If I had a bit of bread, I'd give it to him. Then I'd leave him feeding along the road and I'd go along to the next house. He'd watch me and when he saw me coming out, he'd come and stand at the gate because he was expecting the bread. That's the way I trained him. If there was sweet grass along the road, I wouldn't bother with bread. Tom'd keep eating, and I'd keep going to me houses. Even if they were in a bit in a field, Tom wouldn't leave the road. Nobody could believe he was that cute. That pony was like a fairy, he was so clever.

As winter set in, they returned to the outskirts of Belfast and in early February 1947 their first child, Mary, was born in the Lisborn Road hospital. There was a twin, a boy Nan named Francis, but he died. Two months later, they began travelling again. While Mick mended pots and worked with farmers, Nan sold her "swag" and collected farm produce. Having a baby helped. Farm wives gave even more willingly to the attractive red-haired mother who now came to their door.

THEY WERE very good-hearted people, the Northern Ireland people. If you had a baby in your arms or any children running after you, they had all the pity in the world. And if you brought the children out on a wet day, they'd take them into the house and dress them—they'd give you clothes for the children. And when they'd give you food, they'd give you plenty of tea, sugar, and jam. It was an awful country for jam—the North. It was all orchards, plum trees, apples. And they'd give you pots of jam and lovely marmalade.

But there were also mishaps and close calls, most involving Tom.

WE WERE poor, and Tom was the only independence we had. He was the only way we had of travelling, of carrying our camp around, and if anything happened to him, we'd never get on. One time we almost lost him in Lisburn. There's great land in the North, Sharon, then again parts of it are boggy, very boggy land. There's places they call the "shaking scraws"—the scraw of the land shakes and underneath it's all water. Well, we put Tom out in a farmer's field one night. But when we went out in the morning to get him, we couldn't find him. The rest of the horses was over on a high piece of ground, and we thought Tom must have getting out of the field. So we went round looking, and then we found him.

His poor head was just out of the swamp, and the Travellers we were stopping with got ropes and two other horses to drag Tom out, but they couldn't get in far enough. So we went to the farmer, and the farmer had chains and a tractor. He got in and caught Tom be the neck—you couldn't get around him anywhere only around his neck—and dragged him out. The poor thing. It was good warm weather and only it was, or Tom would have dying. He was there for three days before he could get the use of himself after being all night in the swamp. Many Travelling People lost horses in swamps. We got him grain and we got him hot drinks and we brushed him down and got plenty of blankets. We had to sweat it out of him. Then we got the vet out and he looked after him. We had to pay the vet. The farmer didn't want us to stay in this place, but he couldn't put us out of it on account of the animal. The police from Belfast came out and said, "No, you can't shift them." So we were left there for a week or two weeks until Tom was able to travel again.

We went on travelling then. And one day, on we comes and pult in on the side of the road where we seen a track. "Ah, this must be all right," Mick said. "There was Travellers staying here. The farmers won't mind us, we'll pull in here." So we did. But we didn't know that an awful lot of Travelling People were after being there, the rough sort, the Travelling People that used to do the damage. They'd go into people's hedges and pull them up and burn them for firewood. They'd let the horses in the fields, tramping down young oats and all. We didn't know they were after doing all the blackguarding to the farmers. The poor farmers was persecuted.

The next morning I got up to get Tom but I hadn't nowhere to go because he was standing at the back of the tent half asleep. I walked down the road a bit to get a few sticks to light a fire to make a kettle of tea, and the next thing I seen all this beet scattered along the road. The farmers in the North used to have loads of beet for making sugar. It'd be piled up in sacks along the side of the road waiting for the lorry to come in the morning to bring it to the factory. Well, when I seen all the beet, I turned around and started running. "Mick!" I roared. "You'd better get up quick and get out of this camp before we get kilt in it."

"What's wrong?"

"The horse has all the man's beet destroyed, and we'll never be able to pay for it." Tom was like a barrel, he was that swelled. And if you seen the way he left that beet—any sack he didn't eat, he tore it open with his hooves.

But we didn't get time to get out, Sharon. The farmer came running down the road and a gun with him. "Ah, now we're done," said I. "Here's the B-Specials, Mick. We're done for. Here's the *gammy feens* coming."[20] The "bad men" I called them because if you done anything, they'd kill you. Great big farmers' sons. Oh, the B-Specials would beat you to death.

"You tinkers!" he roared. "We're after getting enough of yous. What your dirt is after doing here the last time."

"Mick," I said, "you're going to be shot."

"Yous dirty tinkers!" roared the farmer. "Look at what your horse is after doing. Come down here till I show you what your horse is after doing." Another farmer came up from the other way and he had a rifle with him.

I went on me knees, begging for mercy. But what saved us, only Mary. Didn't the child start to scream, and I let her scream. I was that nervous, I was afraid to take her up because I thought they were going to put a bullet in me. And they could put a bullet in you for the damages. Mick started to tell what money he had and about tying the pony up at night. He didn't. Sure, he was telling them lies. And Tom was a robbing horse anyway; he'd jump anywhere.

"Go over you and take up that child. Don't be one bit scared," the farmer said. He started talking to us then. Mick told him what they were after doing for us in other parts of the North.

"You can find out now," Mick said. And he gave him some people's address where they'd helped us. "I'd always help the farmers. I'd never do any harm. But this horse, I'll have to get rid of him. Go on, shoot that horse!"

"You won't shoot that horse!" I screamed. "I'd rather if you shot meself." And the screams of me over Tom. I nearly lost me mind.

"Go back and take up the child," the farmer said.

"I won't," I said.

"Are you not going to take up your child?" The Northern people had all the pity for a child.

"I will when you leave down your rifle."

"We're not going to touch your horse," he said. He felt sorry for us then. "You needn't leave here but will you tie up your horse tonight?" So Mick tied up Tom, and they gave us hay to give to him.

That night the farmer came up to us at the fire and he gave Mick plenty of jobs to do. He said good night then, it was about eleven, and away with the farmer. But wasn't Tom getting hungry. You could never tie this animal up; he'd cut the rope with his teeth. Well, the farmer wasn't in his gate when Tom came galloping after him, running at him with his mouth open. Then he gave one jump and right over the farmer's wall into the backyard. The farmer and his son had to get him out. They didn't blame us then. But Mick had to spancel Tom, get a bag and tie his two front legs together as tight as anything. That was the only cure. Oh, we got an awful time with Tom. We got in terrible trouble over him. We'd have to fly in the middle of the night.

But sometimes Tom brought us luck. It was coming winter one time. It was a bad time to be in the country, but we stayed out anyway. We pult in this back road outside a little place called Newtownards. The houses was a bit far away and the village was about two mile. There was a big beech tree growing on the side of the road and we pult in next to it. This tree was beautiful, the shelter of it, and we put our tent in against the back of this tree. It was a lovely evening, a grand, calm winter's night. We went to bed about eleven.

In the morning Mick looked out. "You needn't bother getting out," he said. "Look!" The tent cover was stuck down. And what was it? Only snow. In the end, Mick managed to get out and scrape away the snow. We had some money, so away with me to a shop to get a few messages [food], not thinking of getting much only what'd do us that day. But didn't it snow again. I think it kept snowing for about three weeks. I walked in and out through the houses selling and going to the shop and buying a bit of food, until the snow got too high. It got too heavy then for me to carry the things back through the snow, so Mick went on himself. He couldn't bring the pony or car because you'd never get the pony travellin'. So Mick put Tom into the field.

A farmer came down and said, "It's very bad weather to put that pony in the field. Come up to the house and get that animal hay." And he gave us ropes and ropes of hay, and Mick threw it in to Tom. He even gave us some oats.

"But it come that bad, the snow, that we couldn't get from the tent to the far side of the road. The snow was as high as the tent, only the tree kept a lot away. We'd have been smothered only for the shelter of that tree. Finally, the farmers had to get a plow and plow in to us. It was the heaviest fall of snow for twenty year—the winter of 1947. It was in the papers for years after.

Well, the farmers had all the pity for us. They brought us down food. We had run out of the bit of food we had. They came down with milk, even dinners. They used to plow down and give it to us. This was every day. Finally the old farmer man said, "I'll tell you what you'll do. Get whatever blankets you have and come up and leave the camp there because you'll be smothered. Come up into my shed—the hay shed." He took us into the hay shed and he got a bucket with turf. "I won't put coal in the bucket on account of the baby," he said. "It'll smother its chest." So he brought in red buckets of turf and warmed up the big shed and let us lie in the straw with our blankets. They made us a great place. Oh, it was lovely. "Don't worry," he said. "We have plenty of food here. We'll never starve." And he gave us food.

"I have a couple of pound," Mick said. But the farmer got insulted, very vexed.

"No," he said, "we have plenty." And they went and got Tom and put him into a stable with hay, water, and potatoes. They done for the pony as they done for us. And they kept us there until the snow started to go off.

Mary was about ten months old that time. And with the heat of the fire didn't the snow start to melt and down off the shed it fell. Mary let out a roar with the fret of the snow and said, "Mama." That was the first time she speaked. The woman of the house was in giving us a big pot of tea. "Was that child speaking before?" she said. "No," we said, "that was the first time." We were delighted. They were the luckiest farmers we were ever with. We waited there for three months after that. The snow was well gone. Mick took the basket I used to sell out of and he went all around the houses selling little pictures, hair combs, strainers, scissors, needles, thread, nearly everything you could mention . . . shoe laces, polish. I didn't go out. I stayed with Mary and I was expecting again. Mick was great at talking, he'd get in better with the people than I would. And all the people thought, "These is the two poor people from down the road that was caught in the snow." And the farmers gave him a whole load of pots to mend.

It came a Saturday, and we decided to leave the shed. So we went to the house. "We're going down to stay in the tent," said Mick.

"You have time enough," said the woman of the house. "Stay where yous are till Monday." It came Sunday then and me and Mick were talking.

"I'd love to go to Mass," Mick said. But he was afraid to

say anything because we were in a Protestant part. But didn't
your man hear him.

"What did I hear you say?" the farmer called in. "Do you
want to go to Mass?"

"I'd love to go to Mass," said Mick.

"Well, your church is five miles away. We're going in. If
you're ready in a half an hour, we'll give you a lift," said the
farmer. So Mick got ready and in they goes—the farmers,
three of them, and Mick. They drove him right in and left
him outside the chapel gate. "Now," they said, "when you're
done, we'll pick you up. Wait outside the chapel gate." And
they carried him back. The Northern people were very good
people. When we left, we thought they were the only people in the world they done that much for us and the pony.

Nan and Mick stayed in the North. Two more children were
born: Joe in February of 1948 and Sally eleven months later.
Both were born in County Down near Downpatrick, a prosperous market town set in the midst of gently rolling hills
beside the Quoile River.

JOE was born in a old house outside Downpatrick. It was
bad weather again and the farmer let us into this idle house.
Me brother Joe was with us. And this day Mick and him went
off. They used to have a great time hunting rabbits and selling them. Nearly all the farmers would take two. Well, I took
bad. I never used to keep a date—the time I was supposed
to go to the hospital. I didn't know meself. I'd always try to
get to hospital, but I used to be taken quick. Well, I had no
one around, and it was four or five mile to where the nurse
lived. She lived in a little seaport place—Killough. I was
walking up and down this old house, praying for them to
come back with the rabbits. It was coming stormy and wet

outside and all the cattle were coming round the house, trying to get in. In the bad weather the cattle used to make for this old place for shelter. But what had Mick done? He'd nailed up the front door and stuffed it with rags so the wind wouldn't get in. We used to go in and out by the back door. Well, I nearly panicked. I looked out through the window and all the cattle and the bull with them were shoving their heads into the back door. I didn't know what to do. "I'm done!" said I. And the cattle were tramping, tramping, tramping against the door.

The next thing, thank God, I heard the dogs. "They're coming now," I said. We had a couple of greyhounds and terriers. And when a cow sees a dog, they follow it. The dogs were tearing the cattle away from the door. Mick and Joe came in then and I gave out hell to them. Only for them and the rabbits I could have been dead. "You'd better go quick for a nurse," I said. So out went Joe rushing to get the pony to get the nurse. But Joe used to be very nervous at night, and he came back.

"Mick," he said, "you'd better look for the pony yourself. I'm not able. I'm after getting a pain in me heart." He was afraid to tell Mick anymore. We'd heard that this house was haunted, and what had Joe heard, only the chains of two old goats outside. The farmers used to chain their goats together—their two front feet or by the neck. Didn't Joe think it was the devil or a spirit in the house.

"Stay here then," said Mick and he went out.

"Go out!" I screamed. I was afraid the baby would be born and I didn't want Joe there. "Get out quick," I yelled.

"All right," said he. "Wait for me, Mick." And he ran out the door.

"By the time you get the pony, I could be here with the nurse," said Joe to Mick. Joe was a runner in the Army; he was a great runner.

"If you run down that road, she could be dead by the time you get back," said Mick. But Joe took off running anyway, as hard as he could. Mick yoked up the pony and followed him, but he couldn't catch Joe. Joe got the nurse, and she was on her way back with Joe in her car, when Mick was only half way going.

"The nurse is here now," said Joe to me, "everything will be all right." And he stepped back out the door. It was pelting rain.

Didn't Joe think the nurse would let the car door open so they could sit in. But she locked her door. She left Mick and Joe standing against the side of the house in the rain, and they were soaked.

"You can come in now," the nurse said. "You have a lovely new son." But Mick didn't care whether he had a son or not as long as he got in. He and Joe run in and didn't even look at the child.

"That's a right old bitch, that nurse," they said after. "She locked us out, wouldn't let us into her car." But she'd forgotten. The nurse did tell them she was sorry. Well, that was the time Joe was born.

Sally was born five mile away, about eleven months later. We had a nice wagon then and were camped just at the edge of the village. I was washing out me clothes and then I took a bath. All of a sudden, the baby started to come. I just had bare time to run in the wagon it happened so quick. Mick went off to get the nurse, but the nurse took a long time. The child was about two hours born when Mick came back. I had her wrapped beside me. She was terrible small. When the nurse came I said, "It's too late now. You may leave me."

"Oh, this is terrible!" she started in at me. Well she fixed me up and she fixed up the baby. "Everything's all right now," she said.

"I'll look after her," said Mick. "I'll put on a good fire."

"I'll be back to see you tomorrow," she said. But as soon as she left, Mick went off.

"I'm going in now to get messages," he said.

"Hurry on if you're going in," I said. And I waited and waited, but no sign of Mick. At first I thought he'd be back but then I said to meself, "He's not going to come." Mick was fond of drink.

The coal was going down in the stove, so I had to get up to put on a fire and I had no water. There was a farmer's house up the road—a stony old road. But I said to meself, I feel strong, thank God. And I picked up two big heavy buckets I had: I better bring enough. I was thinking about the clothes lying around after the nurse going. I had no woman there to help me. So I just piled up me laundry, left it to one side, picked up me buckets and went on. I got the biggest laugh when I went to the farmer's house. I had me coat buttoned over me and I went to the door.

"What's wrong down there," said the farmer. "Is that poor woman all right?"

"Yes, sir. Yes," I said, "she is."

"Had she the baby?"

"Yes."

"What is it?"

"A little girl."

"Oh, that's lovely," said the farmer's wife. "Thank God. Wait till I give you eggs to bring down to her."

She was a very nice woman and she gave me a big bag of food to bring down. But I was beginning to get weak standing there, me two knees was going from under me.

"Them two buckets is very heavy for you to carry," she said.

"Oh, not at all missus. I'm all right," I said. But I was lopsided and I was beginning to get dizzy.

"Any milk or anything else you want? Anything you want, send up for it," she said.

"That's very kind of you missus." And I got me two big buckets of water and the bag of food—having two buckets balanced me—and on I goes. Oh, I was sweating.

I got weak when I got in the wagon. I put on tea, gave the

children some food, got me a nice hot cup of tea and went back in to bed. I fell asleep for an hour then. I felt happy. I was proud to have food for the kids. Mary and Joe was in the bottom bed, and they had a good feed and a lovely fire. I said, "Thank God." And I dozed. When I woke up, I started worrying—what if he comes home drunk? Mick was often wicked. But I put on a big pot of water anyway and started washing the laundry. I spread it out lovely, because I knew the nurse was coming the next morning.

Mick came home late and fell in the bed—he was drunk. But he got up at dawn. "I'm going on to get a load of timber," he said and he went off. He knew the nurse would be around, and that I'd tell her everything frontinst him, about how he'd gone off and got drunk. So he got up early and went off.

Then on comes the nurse. "Oh, you're lovely and comfortable," she said.

"Yeah," says I.

"And you have plenty of food, eggs, and everything. Isn't your husband a great man." There was no use in telling her the truth about Mick, if he wasn't there. It'd be only to torment Mick, to shame him, that I'd tell her. And then me temper was cooled down and all. But the nurse stood talking to me so long that on Mick comes with a big load of timber. The pony was straining with the weight of this timber. "Who did that washing?" she said. I couldn't say that I done it because she'd put me in hospital, into the big hospital in Downpatrick. I didn't dare go into the hospital in case Mick'd go off drinking and leave the other kids alone.

"He did it," I said. "Mick did it. Me husband done it."

"My God, isn't he a great husband to do the wash," she said.

"Yeah," said I.

"The sheets are lovely and white," she said. I used to have me sheets lovely when I was young, Sharon. "Oh, you're a great man Mr. Donohoe. You must be proud of your baby girl. You're a great man for washing them sheets."

"What?" he says. Mick gave me one wicked look to me. "I'll be back," he said and he went off to let out the pony. He took off the harness and put the pony into the field. When she was gone, he said, "How dare you tell the nurse I washed them sheets."

"If I didn't say you washed them, I was landed into hospital," said I. "I had to say you washed them."

I didn't feel happy having me children so quick, Sharon. I didn't like the idea of it at all. The babies used to be so young—there wasn't much time between my children—I used to feel sorry for the younger ones. And I got it very hard to manage. It took all me time to wash and clean for the ones I had, and then another new baby would come along when the other one wouldn't even be walking. It wasn't the Travelling womens' wishes. We had to put up with it. If it went by the women, we wouldn't have had a lot of children. But we could do nothing about it.

A woman'd have a baby there in her arms and she'd get up in the morning and carry that baby with her all day. Wherever she went, she'd have that baby in her arms up till it'd be nine months old. Some woman would carry a child till it'd be twelve months old. Some of the Travelling women were big strong women but more of them was very delicate. Still they'd always have them children, carrying them everywhere with another one barely walking by her side. She was lucky if she had an older one to stay at home at the camp and look after the younger ones. The only way we used to manage was if there'd be lot of Travelling People together, and there'd be a couple of young girls there that wouldn't be going anywhere. We'd ask them to keep an eye on the kids till we'd come back, and they would. They'd always help. One Travelling woman would always help the others. The women got it very hard to get their kids reared. We had terrible trouble and worries.

The men used to be happy to have big families. It was all

the Irish custom, the Travelling People and the settled people had very big families. The men thought that if they had a
lot of sons it would keep their name up. The more sons
they had, the bigger their name family would be, and the
men were very fond of their names. But today, they don't
have such big families. The women just won't do it. And I
think the men now is more fond of their wives than they
were years ago.

Years ago men didn't treat their wives so good, Sharon.
They didn't care how many children they had or how hard it
was on them. Only the very odd, soft-hearted man would
care. Travelling men after they were a year or two married
got tired of their wives and fed up with married life. They
got fed up quicker than the women did because they didn't
want to be tied down. Travelling men want their freedom all
the time, they don't want nursing or looking after kids.
Sometimes they'd keep an eye on them—on the ones from
about two year old, the ones that'd be able to walk, but not
the babies. But they wouldn't do it every day for you, maybe
just one day in a week. When the women would come
home from selling, the men would get up and go on. They
wanted to go here and there, to fairs, pubs, pictures, or
whatever. The women have more of a say now, thank God,
but years ago they had no say.

Still, sometimes I'd get me own back. One time me and
Mick were in Belfast with me younger sister Maggie, the
Lord have mercy on her, and me brother-in-law Richie. Rit-
chie used to play the strong man at fairs and all, and he had
to dress up well for his act. He wore a big leather belt, one
of those silver-buttony belts, and leather clothes. He had to
be dressed up in all these grand clothes to draw the eyes of
the people to get money. Richie was a big man, although he
wasn't tall. He was about the one height as Mick—mid-
dlin'—but he was a stout, well-built man. Mick was very thin
at the time. We called him "Micky Thin" because when he'd
stand next to Richie, he'd look so thin.

At night Richie would get all dolled up in these leather clothes, and he and Mick would go off. They used to love to get away. "We're going to the pictures," they'd say. Instead, they'd be off to a pub to enjoy themselves. Then they'd come back and torment Maggie—they'd joke and say they were with women. And so they used to go off with women behind our backs. Well, Maggie really was jealous and she had me tormented.

"There, they're gone now," Maggie'd say. "They're gone, now. Look at them going!" I couldn't get me work done with her going on about Richie and Mick.

"Why don't you go off with them," I said. But men didn't bring their wives to pubs that time, they'd rather get away on their own.

"They're going off to another place tomorrow night," Maggie said. And she kept going on about Richie and Mick.

"Now, I was very fond of sewing, Sharon. I used to love of a summer's evening to get them away, so's I could sit down and make quilts or clothes for the kids. And if I wasn't sewing, I'd be washing or baking or something. So I used to love to see them going off, but Maggie would be annoyed. And she was driving me mental. "I'll put a stop to this," says I. "They won't go anywhere tomorrow." And I was thinking of a plan.

I was after telling Mick several times not to upset Maggie, but no listening. So the next day I got up and I said, "I'm going into Belfast. I have to get a bit of shopping." I used to go to Belfast of a Saturday to get meat and things for Sunday. All the Travellers used to buy meat for Sunday, to have a good Sunday's dinner. So Mick drove me and Maggie in be pony and car. Richie was gone in hours before us to do his strongman act in the middle of Belfast. He used to do it in the green in Smithfield.

Me and Maggie did our shopping. I was just after getting some meat, when I come to another butcher shop and seen this funny meat in the window. "Come here, Maggie, there's real cheap meat," I said.

"Oh," she said, "I wouldn't like the color of it, would you?"

"I would," said I, "I like the color of that meat." It was a bluish sort of meat.

"Didn't you get enough of meat?" she said.

"I did, but I'd like a bit of that. Come on in, we'll get a couple pounds of that," I said. I was thinking of what I was going to do to the men but I didn't tell her. Not till I had it done. I went in and I asked the butcher, "What sort of meat is that? Is it lamb?"

"No," he said, "it's nicer than lamb again. It's young goat."

"It's very blue looking," I said.

"Yes, it's young goat," he said.

"How much is it?"

"Oh it's only cheap. Do you want a few bobs worth?" he said.

So I give him three shillings—you'd get a whole paper of meat for three or four bob that time—and he gave me a load.

"I won't eat that," said Maggie.

"Well," said I, "the poor dogs will eat it if you don't." And I picked up me meat and then I slipped away from her and went down to the chemist. I was thinking if I got a load of castor oil or Beecham's Pills and made a stew, that it'd make Richie and Mick sick so's they couldn't go to the pub. It was a Saturday, and Saturday was the big night and I knew they'd be wanting to go off. So I went in to the chemist anyway and I got a box of Beecham's Pills. I think they were only about six pence.

We went home early. It didn't take us two hours to do our shopping. Richie came home with us, real happy. Said I, "I'll put on a bit of dinner now, while you are making your tea." When we'd come home from town, we'd always have tea and a bit of cooked meat in sandwiches. Said I to Maggie, "You get the tea ready." Then I got me back turned and I didn't let them see the meat and I chopped it up real small. And got a load of carrots, parsnips, onions, everything I could think of, even Oxos [beef bouillon] and I let the two men see me putting the stuff in the pot. But I didn't let them see the meat going into it.

When it was boiling, Richie said, "Oh, that smells lovely."

"Yes, Richie," I said, "and it will be nice too."

Me sister Maggie was expecting a baby then. So Maggie said, "I'd like a bit." But I shook my head. "I'll eat a bit," she said.

"No," I whispered to her, "don't. I have a lovely bit of steak here. I'll fry it when they're gone."

"Give us some stew," Richie said. He was real happy and so was Mick.

"Ah," said I out loud, "we'll give it to the boys first. We'll have ours after." And I packed a big deep plate for them.

"Oh, give us another bit of that," Mick said.

Now, on the weekends in Belfast, the settled people—boys and girls—would all come out for a walk where we were camped. It was nothing only a plain, all grass, and this narrow road. There wasn't a hedge or a tree that you could change your shirt behind.

"It's time, Mick," said Richie. "We'll go in to the pictures." Then Richie gave one jump and away with Richie. Then Mick gave a jump. Didn't they make a run to get to the toilet. The Beecham's Pills were working quick with the hot stew. But there was no where to go to for a toilet, and the boys and girls were coming along the road and they stood there looking after the two men. They thought they were fighting because one ran after the other. So they stood on the road watching: "They must be fighting."

The next thing Richie jumps over a ditch and down into this hole, where it was all a dirty old swamp. But in with Richie, and Mick after him. They were about two hours in

the swamp before they could come out, and then they
couldn't come out on the road. They were ashamed because
of the people from town. So they walked along the fields till
they came sneaking out at the back of the camp. The people
were all gone then. No one was there only me and Maggie.

They had to go down to a pump then. There used to be
big old metal pumps at the side of the road that time. And
they had to pump and pump and throw water up on top of
one another till they got the clay and muck off. They weren't
in form to go anyplace then, to pubs or any place else.
When I told Maggie what I'd done, she got angry. But we
kept that secret; we had to or we'd have been kilt. And Mick
didn't find out. It was only when I got old, I told it to him.

Not long after, Nan and Mick returned south. They traveled
around Bray, in county Wicklow, and then settled in Dublin
for the winter. And it was there that they lost their luck.

V I

Never The Same After

Nan was thirty years old when she left the North and the mother of six, although only Mary, Joe, and Sally were living with her. By thirty-four, she was the mother of ten. John was born soon after her return to Dublin; the next year, Willie; in early 1953, Michael; and twelve months later, Eileen. They camped in a barrel-top wagon in a field in Cabra, on the north side of the city. It was an isolated spot, near a small winding river, and most of the time they camped alone. Nan stayed with the children everyday except Saturdays when she went into Dublin to shop. But Mick went into the city often and before long he was drinking heavily, returning late a night to fight with Nan or not returning at all. Nan couldn't have antic- ipated, or perhaps even prevented, what followed, but her "life was never the same after."

"Mick was going on very bad, Sharon," Nan began to explain. We were huddled in front of the tiny coal stove in her trailer. It was a bitterly cold evening in February. Rain lashed against the side of the trailer, and the blanket Nan had nailed inside to cover the broken front window billowed like a woolen spinnaker into the room. "He'd leave me and the kids," she went on, leaning into her cupped hand to light a cigarette, "on a lonely road in Cabra and go off. He mightn't come back for days. Thank God I had a wagon and I had a stove and I could go out and pick wood and keep the fire going. Mary was eight and she was clever; she'd mind the children so I could get to a shop or some houses to beg."

WHEN MICK did come home, he often give me a beating. I don't know, Sharon, but when Mick'd get drunk, a feeling come over him that he'd like to give me a kick. Somebody told me brother Pat about the hovel I was in and when he heard what Mick Donohoe was doing, he got a mad fit and landed in Dublin. And that very day I was out begging. Mick had taken me money and the only thing I could buy was a little bit of food for the kids. And I had the best pair of black eyes.

That night I put the children in the wagon to sleep, and I put out the lights and the fire and crept under the wagon. I was sleeping underneath it, only I wasn't sleeping, I was sitting up. And me heart was out of me mouth waiting for Mick to come and give me another beating. But who pult in beside me? Me brother Pat, but he didn't let me know he was there. He pult in the road a bit below us and that night he creeped up and he listened. He waited there until Mick came home full of whiskey and brandy yelling, "Get out, you Mullingar prostitute! Get out and go back to Mullingar and take your bastards with you."

Me brother Pat listened but he never said a haypert [nothing]. "Get me my supper, you Mullingar this, you Mullingar that . . ." Mick said—he was going on something terrible— and he started beating down the door of the wagon. He didn't know I was underneath it. All of a sudden I heard this voice.

"Hold on!" Pat roared. "Here's a Mullingar man now. I'm right beside you." And he gave Mick a kitough—a left-handed box.

Well, I got a shock to hear me brother Pat in Dublin. It's a ghost, it's a spirit, I said to meself. Then me brother Pat started sparring with Mick. Mick was young and strong then,

but me brother Pat went up with another kitough and lifted
Mick off his feet. And then Pat gave him a left and a right
and that was the end of it.

The next day, Mick went off early. He got up and got his
things and walked off, through the fields and over the
bridge. Pat got the pony, yoked her to the wagon, and took
me and the children, and brought us down to Mullingar. We
stayed there for weeks. Pat was waiting to see would Mick
come or send me any money, but he didn't. So me brother
rang the welfare about us, and the union man, Mr. Egan,
came down from Athlone.

"Them children's after being neglected. They're after
being half starved in Dublin," Pat told him. "I want me sister's children taken into a home where they'll get their
three meals and get well looked after. I want the boys
brought up as men," he said. "I want them educated so they
won't have to ask anyone what road to follow."

"You're a good uncle," Mr. Egan said.

"I don't want to send away the kids," said Pat, "but I want
my sister's children educated. I don't want them brought up
as dunces. I want them educated so they'll be able to find a
job and read their own names. Look what happened to me
sister because she wasn't educated. And I'll be there, with
the help of God, when them children come out and I'll do
everything in the world for them."

A few days after, me and Pat went to this court and all me
children was sent away. I didn't want them to go; I told the
judge and I told the welfare man not to take them. I was
crying to Mr. Egan, "Have nothing to do with my children!
Don't take my children! My love's in my children. How
would you live if your children were sent away?" But he
wouldn't listen. So I cursed him: "Mr. Egan, I give you my
curse."

He's dead and gone now; he died six year after and left
all his children.

The welfare took the oldest children away first because

they could find homes for them. Mary and Sally, the two little girls, was sent back to Clifden in Connemara. Poor Joe, John, and Willie was sent to Drogheda till they was ten years old, then they were sent back to Salthill in Galway. But the welfare had to wait a month to get a home for Michael and Eileen because they were so young; Eileen was only three months old, and Michael was a year and three months.

While the welfare was waiting, they put the children in the Mullingar hospital—the old county home—and told me they were going to be sent to Strawmullen in county Meath. I went up to the hospital to stay with them. Mr. Egan came to me one day and said, "You can go now and leave your children here. Go back to your own kind, the Travellers, or out to your brother Pat in Mullingar."

"You pig," I said. "You'll never face God. I'm not leaving my children." There was a priest there and he jumped on Egan then.

"Leave her alone," said the priest. "Did you not give her enough punishment by transporting her children?"

I sat down with Michael in the nursery in the hospital, and the nuns was ever so kind to me. The poor priest was kind to me too. "It wasn't Egan's fault, Nan," he told me.

"God forgive me, but my curse and the curse of God go with him," I said.

"Nan, don't curse Mr. Egan. Just offer prayers up to the Almighty God."

"Right, Father," I said and I went into the chapel and cried. I lit candles to our Blessed Mother and I went down on me knees under our Blessed Mother's feet and I cried.

Nan lapsed into silence, her mind far away. My throat felt swollen. And despite the cold rain beating outside, the air felt heavy and implacable. Waves of dim light from a candle by the sink washed hypnotically across the walls. Life seemed suspended, until Nan got up, removed one of the metal rings on the stove, and threw in a few pieces of coal. Then she sat down and continued.

EILEEN WAS sick and they wouldn't let me in to see her, Sharon. They thought I'd carry the infection back into the nursery to all the other children, so I looked through the glass at her. But I got an idea. And a couple nights later, I took me coat out of me locker, put me shoes, coat, and all on, and said to meself, if I can't get Eileen back, then I'll have Michael.

Michael was a lovely little fella, fifteen months old. Oh, he was beautiful. He had real brown eyes and real red curls, and I loved him. "Michael," I said, "I pray God will leave me you."

And what did I do? I sneaked down the hall. I knew the way out. It was about three o'clock in the morning, and I had everything planned two days before. I took four sucking bottles out of the scullery and filled them with milk and put them down me bosom and down me back to keep the heat in. I got Michael and made me way out of the hospital but the gate was locked and there was a watchman. It was like a jail—the old county homes was like jails. I'll have to climb the wall, I said to meself. So I took off me coat and unbuttoned me blouse and put Michael inside and then buttoned me cardigan so's when I'd jump, Michael wouldn't fall out. Then I buttoned me coat real tight. And I climbed the wall no bother. The wall inside was only small, so up I gets and never thinking I said, "Michael, I have you anyhow," and I jumped.

I think I'm falling yet.

From the inside, you'd think it was a low wall, but the drop on the outside was something different all together. I hurted my hip. Oh Jesus, the pain. I don't know how long I was on the ground before I could get up. In the end I walked away. I went the canal way; I didn't go through the town. I got up on the canal and walked until I got to the Dublin bridge. There was nothing then only the main road into Dublin, the straight Dublin road. I hadn't one hay-penny, only a few fags and a few matches. But I didn't care. I walked all night. Everytime Michael would cry, I'd sit down on the side of the road—it was a lonely road, you wouldn't see a sinner on it—and give him his bottle and then I'd go on again. I kept walking.

Come morning I began to get starved. It come on eight, it come on nine, and then it was about twelve o'clock. I was starving but I was afraid to go into a house and ask for a cup of tea in case the guards would be enquiring after me. So I kept walking and when it was about one o'clock I got a lift. This car pulled up, and there was a man and a woman in it. (If I seen a man on his own, I wouldn't ask for a lift because I was always nervous in case it'd be a guard looking for me.) They were only going to Kilcock, but that was good enough, that was very near coming to Dublin.

When they let me down in Kilcock, I went round to the back of the convent and got a lovely mug of tea and plenty to eat, and the nun gave me another bottle of milk. The most thing I wanted was plenty of milk for Michael. I went on again then, starting to walk and thumb lifts for Dublin.

But when I landed in the city I had nowhere to go. So I made for Mick's mother's house but I knew she'd give me an awful eating out on account of the children being taken. I faced her anyhow and I explained to her what happened, but she said, "I can't keep you. I'm not going to keep you." So I was left with Michael in the street.

I went along then, walking the streets until I met a Dublin woman—a woman belonging to the city—and I explained to her what happened.

"Have you no lodging money?" she said.

"No," said I, "I haven't a penny." And so I hadn't any money because I'd been in the hospital waiting with the kids.

"I'll put you up for the night," said the Dublin woman, "and I'll tell you where you can go." Then she brought me into her house and made a place for me and Michael to sleep and looked after us. And the next morning she told me where to go, it was a lodging place for women—the Regina Coeli.

I went in to it for the first time in me life then. I was very glad to have a place to stay, but there was parts of it with an awful lot of winers [winos]. But on account of me having Michael, they put me in a nice part and I was safe enough. I stayed there for a while. And in the day I'd go out begging to a few houses and I saved me money, saving to get me fare. I was thinking that if I got to the North, I'd be all right because I had me sister Lizzie in Belfast and two brothers— John and Joe—travelling in the North. And if I got there, somebody would tell me where they were living. So I saved me fare and made me way with Michael back to the North.

But when I landed in Belfast, I didn't go near me sister Lizzie. I was too badly dressed, too trampy looking. Lizzie had to get her living in that shop, so I didn't go near her on account of the neighbours. I went on walking through different parts of the North looking for me brothers. When it'd come night, I'd ask people for lodging, and when they'd see Michael, they wouldn't let us lie out—they'd put us up for the night.

Well, I kept enquiring and enquiring and when I got to Castlewellan, I met some Travelling People. "Did you see a fellow by the name of Joe Donohoe or John Donohoe?" I asked them.

"Yeah, John Donohoe is in the bog meadows in Belfast. He's building wagons there. And Joe's in Castlewellan, only about a mile away down the road," they said.

I was very happy then. And I went on to meet me brother Joe. I didn't see him for years and he didn't know me first. But he was delighted. And they—him and Olivine, his

wife—didn't know what to do for me. I stayed with them for
near two year. Joe stopped around Castlewellan a lot. It was
a lovely little town with grand places to pull in, and the
farmers was very fond of him. He used to do a bit of work
for them. Joe's wife was a Gypsy girl, Olivine Price was her
name. We used to go out in the morning selling out of a
basket, and she always used to read fortunes. I was very
happy with her.

Well, it come Christmas, and Olivine and me started making an awful lot of artificial flowers to sell for decorations.
She'd make them out of wood, and I'd do so many dozen
with colored paper. I used pink, red, yellow, and white to
suit different sorts of flowers—I used to make lovely daisies,
roses, every sort. The wood ones was colored, too. We had
to buy dye and dye them. Well, on Christmas Eve we went
out selling flowers, and the people were very good. We got
an awful lot of things—biscuits, cakes, money.

We had our shopping done and we were walking home.
We had about four miles to walk to the trailer but what happened? Who did we meet on the road? Only me stepson
Tom, Mick's first wife's child. I got an awful shock. "Where
did you come out?" I said.

"Oh, me daddy and all is looking for you," he said. And
then he told me about the way he'd been walking and how
his feet were sore searching for me. "When me daddy heard
about the children being sent away, he went to Mullingar
looking for you and he got information from Travelling People that you was in the North." Mick had gone to Belfast and
then he and Tom tramped all parts looking for me till they
came round Castlewellan.

When I got to the camp I was afraid that Mick'd kill me
on account of the children being gone. And I was afraid to
go back to him over the drink and beatings. I won't go back,
I said to meself. But Mick took me into the chapel in Castlewellan and he swore to the altar and to the priest that he

wouldn't harm me. He knew it wasn't my fault that the children was gone. Still, I told the priest, "Father, I'm afraid to go back."

"Make a promise you won't beat her anymore," said the priest.

"I won't," said Mick, "only an odd slap if she gets very bad with her nerves. I might give her a slap then but I'll never harm her." But Mick, God forgive him, wasn't a very good believer and he broke that promise.

We stayed with Joe and Olivine for three days after Christmas and then we travelled on our own into different parts of the North. But we got tired of the North and came back down to our own counties, to Westmeath and Longford. And from there we made on to see the children—Joe, John, and Willie in Drogheda and Sally and Mary in Clifden.

I get lonesome and sad when I think of it; that was the end of me little family. My life was never the same after. It was never any good after.

VII

Galway

Dublin brought no luck that winter. After visiting the children, Nan and Mick returned to Dublin and pitched a tent behind a crumbling brick facade in a derelict lot just off the busy North Circular Road. It was noisy, dirty, and wet. Mick kept his pledge, except for a brief binge at Christmas, and left Nan alone, but they had been unable to save much money and by the time spring arrived, they were anxious to leave. They decided to try Galway. Nan was eager to see Mary and Sally again, and Mick—remembering the many small cottages that dotted the landscape—planned to make plenty of money.

But first, they walked to Dominick's, a wholesaler on the Dublin quays. Mick heaped the counter with £10 worth of scrubbing brushes, hair combs, shoe polish, lace, needles, cheap rings, and plenty of holy pictures; Galway was known to be a "backward" and religious place. Back in camp, he carefully spread everything out on a blanket on the ground and priced each item for Nan—a five-shilling picture would sell for ten, a package of needles for three pence. The swag was considered Mick's "work" since he had bought it and any money Nan earned from selling it had to be accounted for and turned over to him at the end of the day.

They left the city in early April, stopping in Drogheda to see Joe, Willie, and John. After that, they proceeded to whatever destination they reached, arriving in Connemara, the

western part of Galway, in mid-May.[21] Around them the land
was a boulder-strewn moonscape, pitted with isolated patches
of grass and shimmering royal blue pools. Tiny white-washed
cottages were sprinkled amid the barren granite like scattered toys on a tiled kitchen floor. The road followed a cor-
ridor of lichen-dabbed stone walls capped in a mosaic of
lavender heather and sea pinks. In the distance the conical
peaks of the Twelve Bens were shrouded in clouds. It was
one of the best times of Nan's life.

WE WERE way out on a country road and everything used
to be lovely. I used to love to pull in beside a bit of a wood
or a river. The first thing we'd do is let the pony loose—take
off his winkers—and let him eat. The next thing, we'd take
down the cover. Then I'd gather some sticks and light the
fire, and if we hadn't any bread of our own, I'd go down the
road and into a house and say, "We're making tea up the
road, can I have a bit of bread." And the farmer lady would
give me a quarter of heavy cake bread. I'd go to two houses
or three, and they'd give me duck eggs and milk. And we'd
sit down then and have a good feed. The travelling life was
the nicest life out years ago.

In the summer, I'd love to be in a tent. Of a summer's
morning, I'd rise up the side of the cover and just let the
sun and air into it. You can't see out through them heavy
canvas covers, but years ago Travellers used to have light
sacks, like calico or twill. It was so light, you'd think it'd
never make a cover but it would. At night you could see the
shadows of the people going up and down the road, and in
the morning, you could look out, just like through a curtain.
When it'd rain, this twill material'd get real close and thick
and you'd hear the rain hopping off it just like galvanized.

When it was raining at night, it was grand and comfortable in a tent because you'd know you were in for the night.

I'd love to hear the wind and rain when I'd be in bed. Michael was gone to sleep in a few minutes. It was beautiful. But I'd be praying for the morning to be good and fine: "I hope when I get up in the morning, the rain's stopped so I can get out and light a fire."

Tents was very warm, you know, Sharon. You could even see them covered with frost. The cover would be all white, but inside it would be lovely and warm. They're far warmer than a trailer or a house. You'd be freezed in a trailer; you need a heater all the time. But not in a tent. The only problem was they were so small, and we were squeezed up. And sometimes I'd be nervous about the ground, thinking was the ground safe. And of a wet bad morning, a tent was an awful place to be. If it was dark with the rain and wind, I wouldn't want to get out. But it was twice as miserable to keep yourself in.

Mick was younger then and he was very fond of trout fishing and eels. He'd go down to the river in the evening time, and I often sat down and waited till ten at the river with him. Then I'd leave him and I'd go back up and put Michael to bed. It was often two in the morning before Mick'd quit fishing. During a moonlit night, he'd come back with a whole hank of fish. And if there was any poor labouring people in the cottages—maybe the husband was only in a small job—we'd give them some of the fish and eels. I was happy at that. It was a lovely life.

I think it was the only time in the world.

I remember me first day calling. I was driving the pony and cart and I was wanting a village so I could start to sell. But I seen nothing, only cottages. Then I seen this old farmer in the road above. "Where's there a village," I asked him.

"There's plenty of villages round," he said. But what he meant was houses. Well, I wasn't used to this because around Dublin or Westmeath, a village is a shop or a couple of shops. But what they meant be a village in Connemara was a village of houses. So I went on to the first little houses and wheeled in and started selling.

The very first house there was four women, but I didn't know. So I stood at the door and called, "Is there anybody here? God save all in."

"God save you," a women answered back.

"God bless you, ma'am. Could you give us a bit of help?" I said. "Any little help you could give. I have some lovely things here." I went in then and spread me things on the floor trying to sell, and they all got round me and started gabbling like turkeys to themselves in Irish. I sat there like a fool; I couldn't understand them. They'd speak English asking me how much something was, then they'd give out to themselves in Irish again. I thought it was the ignorantest thing that ever could be done. I felt like hopping me basket off one of their heads.

And they were picking all me things up.

One woman took up two lovely little holy pictures and hung them on her wall. "I'm keeping them," she said. Well, Mick wanted a pound for them pictures—ten shillings each—because he was after paying five shillings for them in Dublin. So I told them. Another woman said in English, "Oh no, we haven't that money." Five or ten shillings in Connemara was an awful lot that time.

So out the first woman run and brings back three potatoes in her hand, a turnip, and two big sods of turf. She wanted me to give her two ten-shillingy picture for a bit of food and two sods of turf. I never seen anything like it in any other part of the country. In Westmeath, they'd tell you, "Go out to the clamp. . . ." And you'd go out and take a bucket of potatoes or a bag of turf. But there she was with two turfs and the way she held them, they were like turfs of gold.

She handed me the turf and I took it first, thinking she was giving them to me for nothing, along with me money. So I sat waiting for me money and no money coming. The next thing, I says to this one woman, "You speak English. What about me money? I have to get on because I have to be back at three o'clock. I can't be out any later." I'd leave camp at ten and I had to be home at three to get Mick's dinner ready because he would get very cross. And I was nearly an hour and a half in this house and I had nothing sold. "What about me money?" says I.

"She's not giving you any money. She's giving you the food and turf. All our people down here, the tinkers here, gives us those things for food," says she.

"Oh," I said, "I can't give it for food." They all started arguing with me then and I had to go over and snatch me pictures off her wall.

On to another village of houses then, but the people wouldn't buy nothing. They were wanting me brooches and cheap rings but they wouldn't pay for them. All me lovely stuff was going to waste, and if it only got soiled, then I wouldn't get to sell it. Finally, when they wouldn't buy anything, I started to ask them to give me something. I had to beg because I hadn't the money to buy me own food and I couldn't go home without it. But I couldn't ask them for things for nothing because I had stuff with me. So I'd pick the cheapest little thing I had and give it to them, till I had enough of food. One woman gave me two potatoes. Another house gave me a turnip and a head of cabbage. Another house gave me eggs. Another woman gave me a piece of cake bread and a little bit of butter. I was persecuted.

Finally, I gathered up all these little bits and put them in the grub box. The whole load would barely make one good supper. And I managed to buy Mick five Woodbines out of the three packs of needles I'd sold. The only thing I could ever sell in Connemara was needles and tins, because they were cheap. And I got a bit of hay—I used to have to bring home hay for the horse. I got nothing for meself and went home.

Mick came out to meet me. "You must have been going miles today," he said. "The pony is sweating."

"I got fed up and I rushed him to get home quick."

"I'm starving. I'm glad you're back," and he had the kettle boiling. Mick was in great heart because he thought I'd have a pocket of silver. I started taking out me food. "You got plenty to eat," he said. "Did you get any meat?" Mick loved meat and fish. They used to cure their own fish in Connemara. They'd spread the herrings out of a warm day on top of rocks and let the sun and salt dry them, then they'd hang them up inside the roofs of the houses. That fish would do them for one year to the next. But I had no fish.

"No," I said.

"Make me a cup of tea then," he said, "and give me eggs."

I did have plenty of eggs so I made Mick a good feed, and he was whistling and waiting to ask me how much money I made. But I kept moving round, laughing and talking, trying to get him to eat more. "I'll tell you about the money after you eat something," I said. "Here's more eggs and good homemade butter, country butter, what the farmers make." I was scared to tell Mick about the money in case I'd get a kick. And Mick would kick me.

"There's plenty of houses," Mick said, "It's well populated this Galway."

"Oh, it is. It's a beautiful place," I said. "But it's only a scenery place—it's very poor." I was trying to explain to him.

"Did you do any good today?" he said.

"I did. I got plenty of food."

"I'm not talking about food, did you get any money? Did you sell anything?"

"I didn't," I said. "I couldn't get no money, Mick. The Galway people has no money."

"What do you mean?" Didn't Mick think I was making fun.

"They wanted to give me food for all your things," I said.

"What sort of food?"

"They were giving me a saucer of flour, putting it into a paper bag. They were giving me a bit of tea and sugar. And turfs," says I. Well, I could see Mick starting to change. I was afraid he was going to kick me lovely basket of work, and if he did any harm to it, I'd have to pay him back everything. So I said, "I sold three packages of needles and I got three pence each but I had to buy Woodbines for you."

"You were sitting in a house all day gabbing, doing nothing only talking to the people—what you always do," Mick said, "just filling yourself, eating big dinners in the houses. You never went on with that basket at all. Take that basket tomorrow and go the other way."

"I will."

But the next day it was the same. I nearly was crying to the people. The Galway and Connemara people was very poor that time, Sharon. There was some farmers with only one cow and just a calf. A rich farmer would have two. I'd go in and talk to them, and they'd ask me to say a prayer for them, that their son went to America a couple weeks ago. And they'd say, "We're very poor now. We only have one cow. We sold a cow and a calf and a couple of pigs and a chicken to get me son's fare for America, so we haven't much now. Will you pray now that he'll do right?" I'd go on then to another house a couple of miles down the road, and it'd be the daughter that'd gone to America. I didn't know what I was going to do.

Then I met a couple of lovely young girls. "Oh, we're going to England," they said.

"What part?" I said. Then they started asking me where I come from, and when I said Dublin, they got around me. "Did you ever get your fortunes told?" I said.

"No, can you read fortunes?"

"Yes," says I, "I can." This was the only way I could get money in Connemara.

They came out with a shilling first. "Read my hand," said one girl. So I started telling all the lies I could. The other girl gave me a shilling then, and they brought me into their room. "Don't tell me mother. Don't tell me mother," they said.

I went back home then and gave Mick his money. I think it was six shillings I got from selling his scrubbing brushes or something. I put me own money from the fortunes away. I made another good dinner and washed me clothes. "Mick," I said, "you better go on, and I'll start reading fortunes."

"All right," he said. And the next day he went on himself with the basket of work. I took Michael then, and I tied a silk scarf on me head and went onto a little shop and bought cheap earrings—big, long cheap earrings—and all the cheap banglets I could get and bracelets for me hands. And I put on rings. Not one was worth more than six pence. I went on then and got a good few bob. And the people bought things off Mick because he was a better speaker than me. He was satisfied then.

But I'll never forget the fret I got over the fortune telling. I went into this lovely farmer's house, and I was real hungry. The woman had a big cake of griddle bread—it was flat like a pancake and as big as a wheel—sitting in the window. Well, I came in and I was watching this bread.

"Would you like a piece of that bread?" she says.

"I would, ma'am, thanks. I'll have a piece," I said. So she gave me a piece of cake and a lovely mug of tea. The woman blessed herself and sat down. Then she got up and cut me a lovely piece of bacon. They used to hang the pig in the roof of the house after they'd kilt it and they'd cut a piece down every time they'd want to get their dinner. Well, she got a big knife and cut a piece of the pig down and rolled it up and gave it to me. She was a good woman, real religious—she kept telling me to pray for her. "I will," says I.

Then in comes her two daughters. That time in Galway girls used to wear their hair in plaits or up in buns behind like an old woman and they used to wear red flannel petticoats—the bottom of them was done with black velvet—big aprons, and little three-cornered shawls just around their shoulders. The Travelling women dressed something the same, only they wore big black shawls and big black hiker's boots—strong, laced boots with metal tips on the front and another on the heel. Oh, it'd take a good strong woman to carry the weight of those shoes. I never was able for them. The Travellers and the country people dressed something the same. You wouldn't know a tinker woman from a farmer's wife, except that the country woman kept herself cleaner because she had water to wash herself.

Well, these girls was beautiful. They'd been out in the bogs helping their father and brothers cut turf. And when they came in, didn't I start thinking of money. And when the mother went out of the room for something, I said to the two girls, "Why don't you get your lucky fortunes told."

"We don't believe in that," one girl said. "No one can do that, only God."

"Oh, they can," I said, "take a wish and I'll tell your wish." But wasn't the old woman listening to me from the next room. She run in and took up the brush.

"Get out! Get out!" she roared. "There's nobody can tell fortunes, only God. How dare you bring your unlucky words into my house." And she run me out with the brush and set the dogs on me. I had to fly for me life. I couldn't even turn back for me bacon.

I had to go on then, in and out of the houses and beg me food. I was afraid to ask any other girls for fortunes with the fret I got.

When I got back, Mick said, "You're a very bad color. What happened?"

"I'm nearly being kilt over the fortunes. This is religious country and never again will I tell fortunes."

"Ah, some other excuse," he said. "You were sitting down in some house all day." But then I told him the story.

"I'm sick of the fortunes. I'm going. . . . I'm catching the bus for Dublin," I said.

They were a very religious and superstitious people. We had an awful lot to learn back in Connemara. Before they'd give me a drop of milk, they'd get a pinch of salt and put it into the milk. They counted it very unlucky if they didn't. And another thing, Sharon. Salt was the cheapest thing out years ago—you'd get a package of it for a penny that'd last you for months—yet it was a thing that Travellers used to forget. But if you went to a house in Galway and asked for a bit of salt, especially of a Monday morning, they wouldn't give it to you. It'd make them very angry and vexed. They counted it very unlucky to give out salt, and if they would give it to you, they'd leave it on the table and you'd have to get a spoon yourself and put a bit into a paper and take it. But before you could, they'd throw the sign of the cross three times. I never got to the bottom of why the Galway people used to do that. I suppose they had their own meaning, maybe for the good of the souls.

I often went down to a house in the morning and asked for a drop of milk and if I didn't mention the name of God or say, "God bless you" or something like that, they wouldn't give it to me. And in the mornings when they were going out their door, they'd put their hand in the holy water and make the sign of the cross to bring them luck. Well, in other parts of Ireland the people didn't bother with that, they'd just go in and out the door the same as nothing was happening.

Mick was nearly kilt when he enquired the way to Clifden. A bunch of men were standing out in the bog with their bare feet and their trousers wrapped up to their knees. They used to get in making the turf. And Mick run out to them shouting, "Which way do you get to Clifden?" But weren't they saying the Angelus. The very minute twelve o'clock would come and the Angelus would ring, they'd drop mugs, forks, spades, and all and they'd stand up in the fields for half an hour and say their prayers. But Mick didn't understand. They don't do that in our counties, in Westmeath or Dublin. They only say the Angelus to themselves.

When it was over, this big farmer gave out to Mick. We were cleverer after.

Clifden was a lovely little village, a seaside place, and the convent where Mary and Sally was stopping was covered in trees. When Mick and me went there, the Reverend Mother showed us all the different parts of the convent, and the dormitory where the little girls slept. Mary was the pet of the convent, she was a great one for music—the mouth organ—and step dancing. The nuns used to take her every- where—to fairs, to sports, or any place at all, and she had a uniform covered in medals.

"But poor Sally was like a Cinderella. Isn't that right, Sally?" Sally muttered an obscenity and started to say something, but Nan cut her off.

THEY USED to leave Sally in the convent all the time, Sharon. But one night when the nuns wouldn't take her with them, she took all the small children into the garden and they ruined it. They picked all the apples and ate them, and then they went into the storage room and they done all the harm they could, throwing turnips everywhere. And then they let the chickens loose and broke eggs. Well, the nuns put them all in a dark room until they got scared and told who done it. Sally got an awful beating then and from that day, they never trusted her.

Well, Mary and Sally was longing to see me. Especially Mary. I used to write to her and I'd send them parcels at Easter, Patrick's Day, and Christmas—I got them socks and different things. But when we went back to see them, Mary took it very hard and she wanted to go with us. But I didn't want to take her back on to the road or Sally either, because I'd have been doing wrong. They were well looked after and getting an education. So I had to sneak away from the convent, and Mary took it very hard. Sally didn't take it the way Mary did; Sally always walked into life the way it come.

Nan's story was interrupted when Michael walked into the trailer, followed by Mick. As Nan got up to make tea, Sally launched into a tirade about the nuns. I stayed about an hour longer and then walked back to my wagon.

When I went to Clifden years later, I found the convent easily. It sits just behind the town on a hill below the church. I could imagine Nan and Mick wheeling their pony through the imposing silver-painted metal gates, up the tree-lined lane and past the circular lawn to the front of gabled buildings. The days I visited, Sister Aloysius who had ran the orphanage was gone, but another nun—a young novice at the time— remembered Mary and Sally, although she couldn't tell me more. The orphanage closed in 1983 and is now a vocational center for the mentally handicapped. Clifden has changed too. Once a snug market town and fishing port, it is now a tourist center with German, French, and Dutch more common than Irish.

I knew from past conversations that Nan and Mick spent the rest of their time in the West camped on the fringe of Galway City. Mick worked as a laborer on the docks and then in a timber yard, while Nan sold swag and begged from door to door. Kevin was the first child born in Galway, not many months after they arrived. He was followed in 1956 by Martin and a year later by Kathleen—Nan and Mick's eleventh child, and Nan's fourteenth. In eighteen years of married life, Nan had been pregnant for more than ten.

"I was near dying with Kathleen, Sharon," Nan said. We were talking about Galway, and I was trying to get straight which children had been born there. It was a cold, windy morning in March, but clear, and we sat outside next to a blazing campfire which Michael kept fueled with boards and broken chairs.

I DIDN'T get time to have doctor or nurse. She was born in a tent. She was a breech birth, and I was hours in labor. We were way out in the country, although it was the main road, and when they finally got the ambulance, I was just going off. I screamed for the doctor, "Come, I'm dying." He give me a needle, and I remember nothing—the sight and all left me. I remember nothing, only going in the hospital door. It was raining and I was glad to let the rain fall on me face, I was that weak. Kathleen was already born then, they just had to get the rest from me, the afterbirth, and they couldn't get it. I was bad after and I stayed in the hospital for a few days.

I was only after coming out of the hospital with Kathleen, when what happened? I never forgived the Galway people for this. Some of them were good, but more of them—the poor class of Galway people—were very ignorant. They were a poor, spiteful people and they classed the Travelling People like dogs.

We were sleeping at the side of the main road, where all the traffic was. We didn't pull in the back roads, because they were too narrow and there was no room for a tent. You'd have to go miles outside of Galway City to get a wide place to put a camp. We were on the main road, anyhow, and we were in bed. It was a Saturday night. I had a little cot in the back of the tent for Martin. Michael and Kevin were sleeping next to it. And I had Kathleen, she was only eight days old, sleeping in me arms to keep the heat in. There was two babies, a year between them.

It was about two o'clock in the morning when we heard these screams. I didn't know what it was. Sometimes if a whole lot of Travellers got drunk, you'd hear them fighting and screaming among themselves. So I said to Mick, "It must be a lot of strange Travelling People that's drunk. If they come here, they'll kill us when they don't hear us speaking like them." I got nervous because we weren't

belonging to Galway. And the Galway Travellers were
rough—a different breed altogether towards us.[22]

"Don't worry," said Mick. "There's nothing we can do. It's
too late, anyhow. Travellers wouldn't be screaming at this
hour in the morning. If they had a fight, it was all over by
now. I wouldn't be scared."

But this screaming kept on, Sharon, and what was it? Only
a whole crowd of boys and girls coming home from a
dance. Respectable farmers' sons and fine young girls—
some of them had priests belonging to them. But there they
come down the road, and I wouldn't like to mention the
language of these boys and girls screaming and laughing at
us: "Oh, there's tinkers. We'll put them out. Come on, we'll
run them. Come out, you tinkers! Come out! Come out or
we'll beat you out!" And the next thing in comes big stones,
big rocks fired in on top of us. I did get scared then and I
started screaming meself. I had to creep out on me knees
with Kathleen—the tent was only small—begging for mercy.
"Don't fire the stones, the children will be hurted," I said,
telling them how many children I had in the camp.

Mick got out the other side, but what could he do? If he
made any offer to run at them, we'd have been kilt. So we
stood there facing them, praying and begging them to let us
alone. The rocks were coming down everywhere. The next
thing, they let loose the pony. We had the pony tied to the
hedge down the road a bit. And they started whipping the
pony—you could hear her roaring.

Finally, they quieted down. It was a cold night and the
rain was coming down. The tent was all knocked down, only
the cover saved the children from getting a belt of the
stones. I runned to get little Martin. The next morning he
had a cold in his chest, and Mick had to carry him into the
clinic. He was a beautiful child with lovely golden hair. The
doctor said, "I think your baby has pneumonia." So they
held him in hospital and he was a month in hospital. Kathleen was kept in with her chest too.

I kept going in to see Martin and after seeing him for a while, the doctor said, "We're going to keep him in longer. We think there's something wrong with his little brain. Did he get hit in the head?"

"No," I said, but then I told him about the farmers' sons and I said, "They hit the cover."

"Well," he said, "the child's head must have been hit. His brain is damaged. Do you know the farmers?" I didn't know them at all.

Martin was in hospital for months after. Then one morning a wire come telling me to take Martin out of the hospital. So I went in and the nurse was ever so kind to me.

"Come on down. Wait till you see your little baby," she said. "You're taking him home today."

"Yeah," I said and I was delighted—I was thrilled.

The nurse had these little birds that the children played with and she said, "Watch him laugh at the little birds. Look at him smile." But Martin wasn't smiling.

"No," I said. "He's not smiling. The child is very sick. The child is in pain."

"Oh, not at all. Don't be stupid."

"He's not well," I said. But I took him home anyway and I put him in a cot. While Martin was in hospital, Mick built an accomodation—a cover on top of a cart—to get the children off the ground. It only had two wheels, but we had the back propped up to hold it up and it was grand and comfortable, as big as any wagon.

Well, Martin took his bottle but not much. Mick used to be up at six in the morning because he was working on the hammers, widening the Salmon Weir Bridge in Galway. He'd get up and make a cup of tea and give me a cup and he'd make a bottle for Martin and give him his little feed. But this morning the child didn't take his feed, so Mick called me.

"You'd better get up. He's not taking his bottle."

"He must be tired," I said, because he did cry during the night. "Let him sleep."

"No," says Mick, "you'd better get up."

"Take him up and rub his little back," I said. So Mick took him up in his arms, and the child stretched while I was getting out of the bed. He died in Mick's arms.

Well, I run. I think you could hear me screaming miles away. There was Travelling People above us on a lane—Rahoon Lane.[23] And they were sitting having their first cup of tea and they heard me running. I had a good mile to run and it was all up a hill, but I run. They all came up to me, to see what was wrong. They thought that Mick was fighting with me because Mick had a fashion that when he'd be drunk, he'd give me a beating. And I used to run from him. But when they heard me child was dead, they all ran down to the camp.

With death or sickness, the Travelling People would help out anyway they could. Someone went to tell the guards, and the sergeant that came was real nosey: "What happened to the child?" But I wasn't able to speak nor was Mick. We felt it horrible. So this Furey woman told him that the baby was only after coming out of the hospital. The guards went to find out, and the doctor told them that Martin was dying but that they didn't want to tell me. The doctors should have telling me, Sharon. They knew he was going to die and they handed him home to me, to die with me. It was an awful shock.

I took all Martin's clothes and put a match to them. And we burned the accomodation. Years ago the old rule was when anyone died in a wagon, you had to set fire to it. It was too lonely to keep it—the memories.

Well, the Travelling People had all the pity in the world for me and Mick. They got us a canvas and they moved us over to the other side of Galway just so we could forget about Martin. I never went back near Rahoon, and we didn't bury him in Rahoon. We buried him at Bohernmore in a

lovely cemetary. We were poor and the priest arranged it—
coffin, hearse, and all. We had an awful big funeral with all
the Travelling People. And there was a lot of the town people there that knew Mick or that knew me. It was very sad, I
can still imagine that I see the little coffin—a snow-white
coffin.

I always held that in for the Galway people. I hold that in
yet, God forgive me. They were the cause of my child's
death. Ever after when I went around selling things, I let
every Galway woman know that even it if mightn't be her
son, it was a neighbor's son or one not far away from them.
I wasn't long letting them know how me child would be
alive only for them. I think it changed an awful lot of them
towards the Travellers. It did, because all the old women
was talking about it and the priest read it off the altar, about
the bad way Travelling People was treated. It changed them
for a good while after, but I believe not too long ago,
Sharon, Travelling People got a house in Galway and the
people wouldn't let them in it.

After Martin's death, Nan and Mick camped in Menlo, a
village lying four miles north of the city on the east bank of
the broad Galway River. It was a pretty place, the houses
arranged higgledy-piggledy on a series of winding laneways
and hills. Life went on as before except that Mick's drinking
grew worse. Each week he spent more of his wages in a little
pub in the Claddagh, the once distinctive fishing village that
had been swallowed by the city. There he mixed with "town-
ies" rather than Travellers, finding temporary relief from the
isolation and anger that haunts the uneducated and emotionally bruised. The custom of rounds forced everyone to drink
more than they should, since part of the pleasure of drinking
was to be carelessly generous when you could.

Nan claimed that Mick forced her to wait for him in the
pub once her shopping and work were done. Mick was a

jealous man, like most Travellers, and apparently wanted to keep an eye on her. He also wanted her companionship on the long, lonely road back to Menlo. This sounds nicer than it was, since drinking made Mick violent and Nan a convenient target. Nan never mentioned drinking herself during our many conversations, and for long stretches of time she probably didn't. But Galway Travellers who knew them remember both Mick and Nan as "fond of the drink."

I'D WANT to get home with me messages, Sharon, but Mick wouldn't let me go. If I did try to go, there'd be a fight. So every weekend I'd be waiting, sitting in the pub. I wouldn't drink because I was thinking of the lonesome road home and of the children. And the men—you know the way, when men is drunk—kept handing me over glasses of orange. I kept refusing, but still they'd give it to me. I used to be poisoned with this orange.

And I was tormented. I used to feel terrible ashamed. Lucy Dodd, a Travelling woman near us, used to mind the children in the day, along with my Michael. The children would have their dinner and tea got and they'd be in bed when I'd get home. She understood that I had to wait, but it was getting on me nerves. I couldn't put up with it. So this day I told Mick, "I'm not waiting on you this weekend."

"You'd better wait till I'm ready," he said. "The kids is all right. What do you want to go home for?"

"It's not right. What good is it for me to be sitting in a pub with a lot of men? When I get me messages, I'm going home."

"You'd better wait till I'm going, till I give you the order," says Mick.

"I'm taking me own orders now," I said. So didn't Mick hit me a few clouts. We were walking towards the canal bridge going into the Claddagh, but he kept at me. Finally, I gave out to him in the street. I screamed and called him

every name—what I never used to do. I didn't care then
who was looking at me. But Mick kept aggravating me,
answering me back, answering me back, and giving me
clouts. He gave me one clout then and the very minute he
did—he tormented me that much—I left down me shawl
and jumped right over the bridge into the canal.

It's a big bridge, the canal bridge, a very high bridge. But
I got that tormented, in a rage, that I jumped into the canal.
With the luck of God, it was near the Claddagh where the
fishermen was or I was gone. I can swim, Sharon, but with
the fall and the weight of me clothes, I was going under.
And I was in that bad of a temper, I couldn't swim. I was
paddling, paddling, trying to keep meself up but I began to
lose me wind. I wasn't strong enough. And the water was
floating quick after a week's rain.

By the luck of God, this man pulled me out. And when he
did, the guards was there and they brought me up to the
barracks. They were going to charge me but they got a doctor down, and he said it was me nerves. But I didn't think it
was me "nerves." Would you? I didn't see how it was me
nerves when I was after being boxed around and tormented.

Mick was good for a while then. He was nervous of the
guards.

I was going around selling, and one day this young
woman took me in for a cup of tea and asked me life story. I
told her I wasn't all the time on the road and where I'd
worked. I told her about Mick and the way he was going on.

"You're awful foolish," she said.

"What can I do?"

"I'll give you a job here. Would you like to take it?"

"I'd be delighted," I said. "Anything to quit the selling
and begging at doors."

She gave me a job then. I used to have to walk four mile
into me work, down a long stony road. But I didn't have to
be in until nine or ten. She gave me three days work a

week—scrubbing and sewing, more sewing than anything
else. She was a doctor in the hospital where the children
was born. And she had one sister and the father and mother
living with her. They were from that freezing country—Swe-
den, I think—but they were years in Galway. They were
ever so nice, but I really couldn't understand them and they
used different foods than us. I'd bring the baby, Brendan,
and they loved him. I'd had two more babies—Sam and
then Brendan. They paid me well and any roast meat or anything that'd be left over, they'd give me a pack to bring
home to the kids. And I could visit Joe, John, and Willie,
they were living in St. Joseph's Home in Salthill that time. I
was happy enough.

I got another job then. Miss Corbet from the Legion of
Mary came out to see me one evening. The doctor was telling her what a good worker I was and how honest I was.
She used to leave money under me in the house and I used
to sweep it up and hand it back to her. Well, Miss Corbet
offered me a job. "There's a priest's mother," she says.
"She's very old, and I'd like if you would clean up and give
her a hand." The priest was out in Africa, the second son
was working in Dublin, and the other son was staying in the
house but he'd get out at eight in the morning and wouldn't
be back till late at night.

Now, with the three days with the doctor and the three
days with this old lady, I was getting on very well. And the
Legion got real fond of me and got me a lovely trailer. It was
a trailer they used for themselves in the summer but it got a
bit wrecked. So they done it up and give it to me. I was carrying on with me work great and gettin' very well off and
happy, then Mick started in at the drink bad.

This one night it was closing time and we started coming
home on this lonely road to Menlo. There'd be a house
here and then a long way from that, there'd be another
house. And the stony country road used to cut the feet off
me. I was carrying me groceries in me arm, wearing me

black shawl—I always wore the black shawl. Mick started beating me coming along the road, kicking me. There was a dyke at the side of the road, even with the road, and the land was all a swamp—all dirty muck. But anyhow, Mick was beating me and he kicked me right into this muck. Mick seen me go down, but he walked on.

Well, the screams of me. I screamed and screamed and kept catching at the scraws [pieces of sod], but the scraws came away with me. And the weight of me shawl was bringing me to the bottom. An old farmer came along on a bike and he got a bad fret. I don't know whether he was watching his land or his cattle in the fields but the poor man nearly fell off the bike when he heard me scream. And then he was half scared to come over to see what it was. He let down his bike and he said, "What's wrong?"

"I'm drowning, help me," says I. So the poor man pulled me up and got me out. It took that big man an awful lot to get me out; the weight of me was fierce with all the muck. We dragged me shawl out, but I had to leave it. I walked on then and went to the Dodds'.

"What's wrong with you, Nan, at this hour of the morning?" Lucy said.

"Mick thought to drown me," I said.

"He didn't!"

"He did. He thought to drown me, Lucy. A man had to pull me be the hair and then he got me by the hand and dragged me up."

"You're worse if you don't go in and have Mick arrested," she said. "We'll be a witness. Put him to jail."

"No," I said, "if I got him taken, they mightn't put him in jail." People in Ireland weren't for women that time, Sharon. Sometimes the guards would only laugh at you when you'd go in. And they might bring Mick to court but they might let him off, and then he'd kill me.

Well, Lucy brought me in and gave me dry clothes. And she came down with me to the trailer in the morning and told Mick off. And her husband said, "That's not right, Mick."

It wasn't long after, we were coming home again on this lonely road to Menlo. It was a Saturday, and I'd gone in to get messages for Sunday and Monday. I went to the market. There used to be a big market in Galway City of a Saturday with vegetables, eggs, cheese, butter, and all. And I got me basket, a square basket, packed up for Monday. The kids was small so I packed it with butter, tea, sugar, a dozen of eggs, even milk. I had to met Mick at the pub, but I was about a half hour late. When I'd be shopping, I couldn't hurry because I'd be trying to get bargains here and there. If it had of being me own money, I could have got anything I wanted, but Mick had given me some money and when a man gives you money, you have to get more for it. They expect more.

Well, Mick was very contrary. He gave out hell and made a couple of clouts at me. But he couldn't really hit me in the town. He gave up arguing with me till we come to this rail-road bridge at the end of Galway. There wasn't a house for a half mile. Well, Mick made one clout at me, and he got me somewhere in the jaw. Then a kick. Me nerves started to shake. Mick had a good lot of whiskey taken, and I knew there'd be no mercy once he'd start.

Well it started to rain, and I was trying to keep me food dry. We were camped out in the country, four miles from a shop, and I couldn't afford to lose anything. So I was putting up with the clouts, but then Mick started to get worse and I wasn't able for it. Still if I run, he would have caught me. I wouldn't be able to run with me big heavy basket and shawl. And I couldn't lose me food, or the children would be hungry. I didn't know what to do.

But what did I see at the corner of the road? Only horses. All the Travellers' horses was standing together in be a gate for shelter because the night was cold and wild. I was freezing and me hands was trembling and I was thinking what in the name of God am I going to do. I was thinking that Mick was going to try and drown me in the same place as before. But God does wonders for you when you do believe in Him. He did that night.

An awful fear came over me and when I seen the horses, I made a run. I run straight in among the horses, put me foot in the gate, and threw meself up on to a horse's back. The horse gave a bolt and away with me and me basket at a full gallop. It was Fonda Dodd's horse—a very speedy, wicked animal. It was me first time on a horse, so I just held on to the mane.[24] I was going up and down, and me shawl was flying. I was trying to hold onto the mane and onto me shawl because if the shawl went round the horse, he'd trip and I was kilt.

Well, the basket never left me arm, but there was a pound of sugar hopping out down against the road, a loaf here, the meat somewhere else, the sausages somewhere else, and it raining. I couldn't save them. But didn't the horse know his own place at the wagons and when he saw the wagons, he pult in. And when he did, Fonda Dodd was just getting up to look for his horses to put them in the fields because the farmers was in bed.

"Who's running me horses?" he said.

"It's me, Fonda."

"Nan, that couldn't be you." Didn't Fonda get a shock when he saw me. "Come out, Lucy. It's Nan up on the horse."

Lucy came out and she said, "That woman's a fairy. She was drowned the other night and now she's up a horse."

"I never seen the like of it," Fonda said. He held on to the horse and I got off. "I don't know, God is with you or something, Nan."

"For God's sake, Fonda, hide me," I said. "Mick is going to kill me. What am I going to do?"

"You're lucky that horse didn't take your life. What's wrong with you?"

"What am I going to do?" I said. "Mick thought to kill me coming along the road." Then I looked down at me basket and not a thing in it. "He'll kill me now for sure. Mick will never do without his food."

"I'll get me bike and go back and get the food," said Fonda. And he jumped on the bike and took me basket and went back along the road in the rain. He was kind. The sugar was all busted, the eggs was gone, the tea was all right, and he got the rest of the messages he could find.

In the morning, Fonda walked down to Mick and he said, "That was terrible going on Mick last night. Nan could have been killed. She got up on the wickedest horse. It was my horse."

"I can't believe it was your horse," Mick said. But he didn't care.

Some nights, Sharon, I'd hide from Mick in this little chapel in Menlo. Our Lady of Lourdes was outside it and all around was pine trees and when it'd rain, I'd be dry under these trees. We used to go to Mass there of a Sunday— Michael, me, Kevin, and the kids. It was only above where we were camped. When Mick'd come home drunk, I used to run and sleep in behind Our Lady—between her and the chapel wall. Mick used to think one of the farmers was tak- ing me in and he never would have found out, only for Tiny.

Tiny was our little dog. We used to tie him up at night, but this night Tiny was loose. And when I heard Mick com- ing back drunk, I ran away across the fields and out behind the chapel and in behind Our Lady. The children were asleep. It was about one in the morning, and Tiny was watching the wagon. He wouldn't leave the wagon and the children until Mick was landed home.

Duck, Mick's son by his first wife, was after coming back from England and was with us for a holiday. Said Mick to Duck, "I don't know where she goes every night, but the house I get her in . . . I'm going to break the windows and I'm going to kill the farmer that gets her." Mick thought everything; he had a very bad, wicked mind.

"Listen here," said Duck. "Watch Tiny. We'll follow Tiny." Duck was a clever man; he was about twenty-nine years of age that time. So the two of them let Tiny trail their way, and on comes Tiny and walks into the trees. In Mick puts his hand and grabs me out be the head and such a beating he gave me at the chapel gate. I needn't tell you the names he called me and roars about "Our Lady this and Our Lady that."

Many's the day I couldn't get to work because my eyes used to be black.

When I visited Menlo years later, I found the large stone grotto with the statue of Mary about a mile and a half before the village. The old chapel had been replaced with a modern one in 1978 but the large junipers growing around the grotto were still there and sure enough, the two at the back were large and dense enough to have sheltered and hidden Nan. The area today is no longer so lonely and bleak. Modern bungalows and houses with enormous plate-glass windows have overwhelmed the six remaining thatched cottages in Menlo. "Crestwood", a new housing development, sprawls on the hills immediately behind the wall where Nan camped.

ONE DAY I was in camp when this fine young man came walking up the road with Mick. It was me son James. He was reared up and educated. He passed primary and all and he could speak different languages. He'd joined the English army and was sent off to Germany and Aden. And when he got out, he came to Dublin and made enquiries about me. Then he went to me people in Mullingar, and they told him I was in Galway. They didn't know what had happened to me—I got lost to me people altogether—but they'd heard I was in Galway.

Well, I was delighted. I didn't know what to do. James had a few pounds and he spent it with the excitement on the kids—Michael, Kevin, Kathleen, and all. He bought them everything until his money was gone. And Mick was kind to me then because James was there. "You'll get a job down on the docks where I used to work," Mick said, and he brought James down and got him a job. James stayed with us then, bought food for me each week, and gave me a few bob. He saved the rest.

One day James came home and when he seen me, he said, "What happened?" Me face was in a terrible way and I had to go to hospital with three of me ribs broke. Mick had beaten me. "Never mind," said James, "I have an idea. Let him go off to the pub Saturday and, Mammy, you pretend to go to work."

"Right," says I, and me and James planned it out.

"When we get him in the pub," James said, "he'll be with his mates drinking, and I'll get a taxi and have all the kids ready. And we'll get out of Galway."

"I'm going to work," I said to Mick that Saturday.

"What time will you be finished?"

"I'm working overtime," I said, "because this lady has an awful lot of sewing for me to do. But I'm getting extra money."

"Well," Mick said, "that's all right. Where's James?"

"I don't know where James is," I said. "He's off with some of the young fellas from the town."

So me and Mick walked in to the town. "I'll get the messages, and you can take them home," I said to Mick.

"Get eggs," said Mick. He was very fond of eggs. So I got a dozen of these big blue duck eggs in the market and a heap of corn beef. When Mick seen them, he said, "Oh, they're lovely. There's an awful lot of meat there." But I knew he'd be needing it, because there'd be no more shopping done.

"Now, there's your shopping. Look after it and bring it home, because I won't be finished till six."

But Mick said, "I'll take it into the pub and when you're finished, call for it."

"All right," I said—anything to get off. Mick thought he was going to have a right day's spree and that I'd have to take the messages home meself. He was real happy.

"Watch those eggs," he called to the barman. "Leave them there till the missus calls for them." But the missus was a long time calling, Sharon. She never called in Galway for her eggs no more.

I went back to camp then and the taxi came, and we got into it—me, the kids, James, and a few suitcases all packed to get away.

"Speed it," said James to the taxi man. "Put it going!"

"Why?" said the taxi man. "What hurry are you in?" Didn't he get nervous. "I can't go fast, there's too many turns on this road. What hurry are you in?"

"Get going and don't be asking questions," said James. "Go as hard as you can because I'm telling you." We were trying to get away in case Mick'd come. So off we goes. Tiny was running alongside, trying to keep up with the taxi.

"Pull up and we'll bring Tiny," I said to the taxi man.

"Don't mind Tiny," James said. "Keep going." I started crying for me dog then, and the taxi man did get afraid. But we got to the station anyhow, got on the train, and went to Mullingar and into me brother's house. But what happened to Tiny?

He went to the station and he wouldn't leave it. "You know where I seen your little dog?" this farmer said to Mick after. "It's at the station."

"They went away by train," said Mick.

And that's how I left Galway.

V I I

Dublin

A week later, Nan was in the "California Hills." No sooner had she unpacked her bags, than Pat closed the house in Mullingar and headed for Dublin. Nan and James went with him and so did two of his sons. Together they set up camp in an open field overlooking the Liffey River and the spawling Phoenix Park. Dublin Travellers had named the spot, with considerable imagination, the California Hills because of its scenery. It was the summer of 1961; Nan was forty-one.

As soon as they arrived in the city, James signed on the dole and started gathering scrap metal and used clothing. He sorted the first by metal content—copper, aluminum, iron, lead, and brass—and the second, by fiber. The metal was then stockpiled and sold to Hammond Lane, a metal merchant located on a canal off the Liffey. Nan unraveled the wool cardigans James brought back and rolled the yarn into balls. She tore the more colorful clothing into diamonds and squares and then fashioned them into quilts. It took two days of solid sewing to make one: "I nearly went blind," she told me later. James sold the yarn and unusable clothing to rag merchants whose premises were a series of dusty shops in the Combe, one of the oldest sections of the city. He sold the quilts from the back of his cart: seven shillings and six pence for the cotton ones and ten shillings for the heavy wool ones made from old coats.

A few months later, James married Mary Cawley, a pretty, fifteen-year-old Travelling girl. And so the summer passed; James collecting scrap, Mary begging on the city streets, and Nan sewing and looking after the children.

As the days and nights grew cold, Pat returned to Mullingar, but his sons decided to stay "on the road" in Dublin. With James, they began to build winter "shelters", as many urban Travellers do. Just about everything they needed could be found in Ringsend—the city tip located on landfill across from the power station in Dublin Bay. There, amid diving seagulls and other Travelling families, they foraged for packing crates and lumber, remnants of linoleum and carpets, old window frames and broken chairs, tins of used paint, oil drums, and scraps of tar paper. The huts Travellers made ranged from crude shacks to miniature houses; all were roomy—especially when compared to a tent or wagon—and warm. They were also "homely," with wood-burning stoves and walls papered in orange-hued *Arizona Highways* or aquamarine tropical scenes from other picture magazines. Some had a touch of Eastern mystery, the low walls draped with cheap paisley bedspreads that billowed with each caught draft.

James built a hut for himself and Mary, who was already pregnant. Nan's nephew, Chap, built a lovely hut and then decided to give it to Nan. It had three windows, an open fireplace, built-in shelves for the cooking vessels, and a flowered linoleum floor: "It was beautiful. We painted it blue, and I was happy, meself and the kids," Nan told me. But despite the comfort and companionship of that winter, Nan had troubles: Michael, now ten, was beginning to run wild in the city and so was Kevin.

MICHAEL'D go into town and wouldn't come home at night, Sharon. He'd get pockets of money begging, and then he'd go feed himself in the chippers and stand at the shop windows lookin' in at the tellies. I went to the guards different nights and they'd bring him home, but some nights they wouldn't catch him. And the guards warned me, "We're going to send him away the next time." So I give Michael a couple hammerings, but I never could hurt Michael bad. "Someday we'll get a telly," I told him. But where would I get a telly? They were very dear at the time, and the shops wouldn't rent one to a camp or a hut.

When Mick arrived the following spring, Nan involuntarily sighed with relief; Mick would help control the children. Mick was relieved too. It had been a hard winter in Galway, with heavy drinking and none of the comforts a wife provided. He was lonely, tired, and contrite. Nan was willing to try once again and less fearful than she might have been, since James, her brother Joe, and Pat's sons were camped close by.

For a while it worked.

It was while Nan and Mick were camped in the California Hills that Mary, their eldest daughter, returned. At sixteen she had been released from the orphanage in Clifden and had worked in Galway City before leaving for Dublin. She had been in continuous, if sporadic, contact with Nan and now wanted to see her. Both were to be disappointed.

One day I convinced Nan that she needed a change and drove she and Michael in to Camden Street to do some shopping and then across town to the Phoenix Park. We sat on a bench for a while watching the cattle chew and the deer nibble at the lush grass, but it was cold, so we retreated to the car. Michael lounged in the backseat and listened, while Nan sat in front, politely blowing her smoke out the top of the partially opened window, and told us about Mary.

I DIDN'T let on I was living on the road, Sharon. That was the biggest mistake. I told her in me letters that I had a house and I gave her the address of a friend, a Travelling woman who lived in a house over in Cherry Orchard. I did it because I was afraid the girls where Mary was working would find out she was a Traveller and make a show of her, and I didn't want to let Mary down. I'd put in for a house with the Corporation [city administration] anyhow and I thought I'd have it before Mary'd land home. But on she comes to see me.

"One day old Maggie—the woman's name was Maggie—went out her door and she met this girl. "I'm Mary," she said. "I've come to see me mammy. Is she here?" Maggie brought her in to the house and was thinking, thinking of how to break the news to Mary that I was only living in a shack on the road. "This is a lovely house," Mary said.

"Wait now, Mary," says Maggie, "it's like this. Your mammy is doing her best to get a house but she hasn't got it yet; she's waiting on it. The Corporation is getting her a house." Maggie tried to explain everything. "It's very hard to get a house in Dublin," she said, "and you knew your mammy used to be on the road."

"Well, how is it you can have a house?" said Mary. "What difference is there between mammy and you? Weren't you a Traveller?"

"I was, but I put in for a house years ago while your mammy was travelling and didn't get time to settle any-where."

"Where is she then?"

"I'll send me son with you," said Maggie, "and don't get shocked when you see her."

"No," she said, "I only want to see me mother."

So on Mary comes and when she seen the shack I was in, in the middle of a big field, she hardly spoke. I explained to her what happened, and about waiting for a house. Mick wasn't there that day, we were after having a quarrel and he was off drinking and staying at the Iveagh [a men's hostel]. I didn't know what to tell Mary about him, so I said he'd gone to England to see could he get a job and take me over. "If I can't get a house here in time," I said, "I'll get one in England."

"Oh, that'd be a good idea," Mary said.

"Where are you working?" I asked her. And she told me she'd got a job in Dublin working in a hotel and she asked me to come out to see her the next week. "But don't tell them you're a Traveller when you come and dress in your best."

"I will," I said. I had plenty of clothes and I did know how to dress. So the next week I went on out to see her. But when I got there, she kept me standing at the door. I looked in the window and I knocked—she was in the kitchen dressed in a green uniform and she looked lovely— and here she was looking out through the door and she wouldn't open it for me. I stood there knocking and waiting three times before she opened the door. Well, I took it very bad. But wasn't Mary's mind, her nerves, beginning to go.

"Oh, it's you, mammy," she said. "I didn't think it was you, you're lovely dressed. I thought you'd come like a Traveller to make a show of me."

"Well, Mary," I said. "Our Lord travelled before we ever travelled and He wasn't ashamed of His mother. I never wanted to be on the road; I never asked to be on it. Whatever was before me in life, I got. And now it's up to you to make the best of your life. And I hope you'll never be on the road."

"Did Daddy come back?" was all she said. "Did you get any letters from him?"

"No," I said. I didn't tell Mick about Mary because he was drinking and I was afraid he'd go out to where she was working.

"Mammy, I have ninety pound saved."

"Have you? Well, take it out of the post office and put it in a bank. You'll be doing far better because the longer you have it in the bank, the more you'll get. A bank is the best."

"Do you want it?"

"No, I don't." And neither did I that time. I had a right couple pound saved meself.

"All right then," she says, "I'm going to come out to see you next week and then I'm not going to come out no more. But if you go to England, write to me."

"I will," I said. "Are you sure you'll come out to see me next week? I won't come back here to see you then. You can just come to see me, and no one will know our business. And keep praying that I get the house."

But the next thing, on comes a letter to Maggie's house; Mary was gone to the mental—St. Lomans. She was four year in the mental then. When I got the news, I went here, there, everywhere, and told them about Mary being in the mental and how I needed a house so she'd have a home to go to. But still I didn't get a house.

When I went to St. Lomans, the doctor asked me what happened to Mary. "Did she fall when she was small?" he said. And so she did, Mary was knocked down with a cart and got a fractured skull and her shoulder blade broke once. "Well," he said, "it'd be good if you would stay away from Mary."

"But she's sending for me," says I. And so she was, Sharon.

"Well," he said, "I want her to try to forget you, because we have to try to cure Mary—get her well. I want her to get better and get out of here."

"Will she ever get well?"

"She will."

But Mary was very bad. When she used to be getting sick, she'd scream, "Mammy, don't leave me! Oh, I feel it. It's coming in me hands and legs." Then she'd scream. She took a fit one day when she was out with me, and the doctors ran and grabbed her and slapped her. After that, I wrote to her. I never visited Mary no more. She came back to herself then, thank God, and she met in with another patient, a man in St. Lomans. He was only there with the drink and he was young. The patients used to go to pictures and they'd go and sit there and talk to one another in the seats. The next thing—this is years later—I heard Mary was married to him and living in Birmingham.

Mick had left Dublin around this time. Apparently, he had gotten fed up living in the California Hills. He didn't have a job; he and Nan weren't getting along because of his drinking; and he'd argued with her brother Joe. So in April 1963, he left. Nan didn't know he was leaving. Mick simply took the bus into the city one morning to collect his dole and never came back. She waited for him to return but finally decided he'd gone off to drink and in the morning went into Meath Street to do her shopping. There she met two of Mick's friends: "Mick's gone to England—to Birmingham." They thought Nan knew. "But Mick never told me nothing, Sharon. He just bolted every time he got his money."

After Mick left, Nan and other Travellers in Dublin fell victim to an eviction campaign by the Corporation. The number of Travelling People living in Dublin was growing steadily. To the settled residents of Dublin, the roadsides and vacant lots seemed to be teeming with "tinkers."

But as Nan and other Travellers often remarked, "There's nothing in the coutnry for Travellers anymore." Inexpensive, mass-produced tinware and plastics had been chipping away at the tinsmith's trade for years. Farm machinery—the beet digger, for instance—meant there was less agricultural work for Travellers to do, while tractors meant less demand for the horses many of them sold. More farmers were converting to cash crops or pasturage and buying the food their household needed. Consequently, they had less home-grown produce to spare. Their prosperity also meant that more could own cars. And this, together with better roads and bus service, made it easier for farm wives to get into town to shop, eliminating the need for the itinerant peddler. Travellers had little choice but to "shift to the city."

But it wasn't only the number of Travellers in Dublin that bothered people, it was also the way they looked and the way they lived. Their camps were no longer picturesque but littered with car bodies and piles of scrap metal being stockpiled for the foundry. Their winter huts reminded people of far-off poverty in Africa and the slums of Latin America. Begging got on people's nerves. Gone was any pretense of selling; there was no real reason for Travelling women to try, since any housewife in the city could easily get to a shop to buy what she wanted. So women and children begged openly, walking from door to door in the suburbs or sitting on city streets. The image of Travelling People was changing; the hardy rural vagabond, the honest tradesman, was replaced by the social parasite, living in squalor off society's back.

As public complaints grew, the city fathers cracked down. Travelling families were evicted from their roadside camps and the land trenched or barricaded behind them. Nan and I had talked about evictions often. Evictions have always been a part of Traveller life, and every family has a repertoire of tales to tell. But in the city, they were becoming more frequent and rough. They didn't affect Travellers living on official "sites" like Holylands. But until the late 1960s, there were no sites and even after a few had been built, evictions remained a problem for every other Traveller living in the city. The "itinerant problem" became the social problem of the 1960s; it continues today.

"Travellers were getting pegged all around Dublin, Sharon. They weren't allowed to stay anywhere—only a night here, a night there," Nan said as we sat in rush hour traffic on the way back to camp.

WITH MICK gone, I was on me own again with all the kids. Michael was eleven then and Eddie, the baby, was three months. One day the Corporation came and gave us a week's notice to get out. Well, I was in a terrible mess. I had nothing to carry me out—no pony, no wagon, nothing, only me hut. Me brother Joe was camped a bit above me. His family got packed up and they went on. But I had to wait till Joe came back with the four-wheeler and the horse to carry me and the kids away. So I was waiting in the field when on comes the Corporation and this bully, "Big Bill" the Travellers called him, roaring, "Come on you knackers, get out!"

"You'll have to wait," I said. 'I can't carry me things and I can't leave me children. I have to wait till they come back with the cart." I was real nice to him, but he was a real brute.

"Tear down the hut!" he ordered his men.

"Don't take it down. Wait till they come," I said. I didn't know it but the guards kept following me brother Joe, and they drove him miles away. Before Joe could come back, he had to find his own place to camp. Well, this Big Bill kept at me, and I was getting nervous waiting on me own. So I said, "Leave the hut up till I get out me kids, me blankets, me pots—just what I'll need." And I went in and started taking out me things. Then all at once, they started pulling down me hut. I got Eddie, the baby, out and all them that was able to walk, but Brendan was still inside. So I rushed back in to save Brendan—he was a very delicate child—and the very minute I did, the boards was coming right in on top him. I just caught him and thrown him out the door, and then the boards came right down on me leg and I collapsed. If it was now, I could have Big Bill locked up and the Corporation sued over it. But the law gave us no say that time.

When me brother Joe landed back, he got a bar and he runned at them. And bad leg and all as I had, I got another weapon and run at them too. Gratton Puxon, the Englishman that was helping Travellers, and his wife came along then and brought me to the hospital.[25] I got me leg dressed and explained what happened, but the guards wouldn't do a thing about it—once you were a Travelling Person there was nothing done. I was three months with that leg, it swelled up terrible, and I have the mark yet. I was near crippled.

Travellers got an awful lingering life, until we started to fight. Me brother Joe, Gratton Puxon and his wife, the students from Trinity College, and the Travellers—we all stood up against the Corporation and the guards.[26] There were some bad fights out in Cherry Orchard; the students and Travellers held on to the wagons and wouldn't let the Corporation in. And the Travellers went down O'Connell's Bridge with wagons and signs. We may thank the students and that Englishman. If it hadn't been for them, we'd have an awful life today. It'd be a worse life.

After I was shifted, the students were great. They used to bring me food to keep me going and they put it on the radio that I was left with so many children, and all the settled people came then with envelopes and left me money. I bought shoes for the kids and I was happy enough in a wagon waiting to get me house. But one night, what happened?

I was in bed—I had a lovely fire going—and it was about ten o'clock, when there was a rap on the door. I didn't know who it was. What if it's a man, I said to meself, and I got scared. But who comes in? Only Mick, back from England. He had his grandchild with him so's when I'd see the child, I'd get soft. I felt like killing him. He was all dressed up. He had about thirty pounds worth of a lovely coat on him and there I was, sitting in a wagon with six children. And he never sent us any support or nothing. Well, Mick took out sweets for the kids, and he was ever so nice. He knew he had to be nice. We started talking then, and I told him all about the Corporation.

"You needn't worry," Mick said, "I have a place for you and the kids in England." And he asked me to go to England with him.

"I won't go," says I. And I wouldn't give in; we argued for about two hours.

"I'll take Michael and Kevin then," said Mick. He was going to leave me Eddie—Eddie was only three months old—Brendan, Sam, and Kathleen. He was going to leave me the smallest ones, while he was going to take the two biggest. I thought it was just as well to go then. I'd rather go than part with the kids.

The next day Mick's daughter-in-law, Nelly Redmond—Tom's wife—came out to see me. "Oh," she said, "we have a lovely place for you in England." I was delighted to hear this because I wanted to get the children a home and get them to school. So I went with Mick. I took clothes, just what would barely do the children, and went. Mick told me not to bother with the rest, that things was cheap in England. So I left pots, blankets, all me lovely things that I'd saved and went on.

We took a bus into the city and stopped at Patrick's Park. Mick went into the pub, while I sat with the kids in the park, and got sandwiches, lemonades, minerals, and sweets for the kids. We waited there in the park until evening, then we walked on, took our time, and got on the boat. The boat wasn't so bad but when we got off at Holyhead, we had to get on the train to Birmingham and it took us hours. We got a taxi then to his son's place.

The slums of Birmingham and other industrial cities, like Manchester, Liverpool, and Leeds, were haven to hundreds of Irish Travellers in the sixties. England's economy was booming, and families bundled themselves aboard the Sealink ferry and crossed the Irish Sea to labor in factories and "on the buildings" and toil at motorway construction. Most crowded into shabby flats and bedsitters in crumbling inner-city terraces like Handsworth, Sparkbrook, and Soho, joining the thousands of immigrant Jamaicans, Indians, and Pakistanis already there. Some took their trailers and wagons and squatted in vacant lots, stripping the surrounding derelict buildings of copper pipe, lead downspouts, and flashing, while collecting unemployment benefits that were generous by Irish standards. England was a great opportunity for most, but it proved to be torture for Nan.

I X

Birmingham

I woke up early and stepped out of my wagon to find the camp perfectly still. It was a Sunday and trailer and wagon doors remained firmly shut. I picked up the water bucket and looked up just in time to catch a fox slinking across the lane. He froze, and we stared at each other for a few seconds before he darted into the ditch. I decided to ask Nan later what seeing a fox meant. Travellers have so many animal omens: chattering magpies presaged trouble, flying cranes foretold a meeting with friends, two magpies and a crow hopping about the camp together meant the police were near. But when I asked her, she didn't know. And as we sat down at the campfire to have a cup of tea, she told me about Birmingham. It was an unsuitably peaceful day for the pain that followed.

WHEN I went over to Birmingham, Sharon, Mick's sons had a big house. Them each had their own room and they gave us one of the rooms—a little room that four wouldn't fit in, and we had eight. We were squashed in it. There was one kitchen, and Mick's three daughters-in-law, the grandchildren, and me own children. One of me daughters-in-law, Alma, was a very nice English girl belonging to Manchester. And then there was Nelly, me daughter-in-law from Dublin, and May—I think she was from Carlow. They were very good to me; the boys was nice too; even Mick was lovely for a couple of weeks.

But what did Mick want me and the kids for? Only money. The first thing he did was take all the children's baptism lines and send them to the income tax. Mick was working in a brewery, and they'd put an awful lot of income tax on him. But by having me and the kids over, they wouldn't stop so much money on him and he'd get all this back money. I didn't know about this until one morning Alma said, "Mick's well-to-do today, Nan. He'll buy you something nice."

"What's different with today than any other day," I said.

"Mick's getting an awful lot of income tax money back," she said.

But when Mick got home, he didn't say nothing about money. And it wasn't long before Peter, his other son, came over, and then the four sons went off with Mick to the pub. They came in late that night, falling everywhere through the door, carrying brown paper bags of Guinness, whiskey, and brandies but nothing else—no food for the kids or anything.

I'd been putting up with this carry-on for a long time, Sharon, but I didn't give out to Mick that night because they were all drunk. But the next morning I did give out to him, and I got a good hiding for it. Mick pegged me from the top of the stairs down to the bottom, and I was carried off to Dudley Road hospital for fractured ribs and me head. I didn't say no more then, I couldn't.

But every Friday it was the same: Mick'd get his money, and they'd be off drinking. It was a hooley [drunken party] every week and a beating for me. May, me one daughter-in-law, used to get hidings too. But that time we didn't know that the welfare in England or the law for battering wives and kids was so good. Mick and his sons had us scared to death to go near the law, anyway. But finally I got that fed up, I said to her, "I'm going to find a place for meself." And I waited for me chance.

I was getting a beating one night—I was bleeding out of me nose—and I decided to run away. But I couldn't go down the stairs and pass them all. So I got Michael, he was eleven then, and he climbed out through the top window and sneaked down the roof to the shed and ran away down to Aston to tell me sister Maggie and her sons to come. Maggie lived about two mile from me.

For the luck of God, Maggie and her sons knocked at the door and took me away. Then they kept me in their house. I wouldn't go back to Mick. Finally I told him, "I'll go back on one condition, that you get me a flat of me own." That was the only thing Mick could do, so he brought me over to Highfield-Smithwick, and we moved into this big house on Vicarage Road. It belonged to an Indian, Mr. Singh. Mr. Singh had a big family and they were very kind people but they didn't live in this house, they just owned it.

First we had one little room; a week later, they gave us another. The boys slept in one, and ourselves and Kathleen in the other. We paid eight pound a week. Imagine! Four pound a room. The second little room was in the attic. It had two beds, but in the winter you'd be freezed to death and it was too near the ceilings. If you stood up, you'd break your head. The toilet was in the back garden, and another one was upstairs. But we used to wash ourselves in our room; I had to bring up water from the kitchen.

I wasn't able to work because Eddie was only a few months old and I had Sam, Brendan, and Kathleen small. Kevin was eight, or maybe nine, and Michael was eleven. Mick'd go to work early, and I'd get up. I could never sleep in the mornings anyhow, so I'd get up and tidy up me two little rooms and get the childrens' breakfast ready—corn flakes, whatever we had—and get them ready for school. I had them washed from the night before, so I'd just comb their hair and get them dressed and off to school. Sam Kevin, and Michael used to go to school. Brendan was too young.

When they were all gone to school, I'd do me washing. The kitchen was at the bottom of the house, and I'd heat big saucepans of water and drag them up the steps and throw them into me bath. I had no washing machine, only a big zinc bath and me own hand scrubber—a wooden washboard. You won't see them now much, Sharon. I used to love to have the kids spotless. The welfare in England was very particular about the kids too, not like in Ireland. The nurse at the school used to check their underclothes, their hair, their hands, their feet—nails and all.

We were interrupted by Brendan and Eddie who ran past and into the trailer to rummage through the cupboards for comic books. Nan took the opportunity to pull a crushed pack of Woodbines from her sweater pocket and dig out the last cigarette. "Eddie!" she shouted. Eddie's face appeared in the doorway. "Run to the shops like a good lad and buy me some fags—ten Woodbines. And buy a bottle of milk," Nan said, reaching underneath her apron into her skirt pocket. "Here's a pound." Eddie jumped down and took the money and raced off through the fields, eager to have a reason to leave camp. Nan folded her lips to get one last drag from the tiny butt of her cigarette, flicked it into the campfire, and resumed her story.

KATHLEEN GOT very bad with her chest when we were living on Vicarage Road. The doctors sent her to a sanatorium miles out of Birmingham. One part of it was a convalescent for children and the other part was for TB. Kathlyn was born with a bad chest, and the Birmingham air never agreed with her. It must be the smoke. What do you think, Sharon? The doctors at the hospital were checking her all the time and then they wouldn't let her back to our rooms and she was sent on to London—to Father Hudson's Home. Kathleen

was there for five year. She'd only come back for three
weeks at Christmas, six weeks in the summer, and two
weeks at Easter.

I remembered that Nan's daughter Sally had turned sixteen around this time and been released from the orphanage
in Clifden. "What about Sally?" I interrupted.

GOD BLESS us and save us, Sharon, poor Sally. Sally was a
mess. She was let out of the convent in Clifden and when
we met her at the station, she was still wearing the convent
dress—a plain cotton dress—and a pair of old lady shoes,
big black laced shoes. And the way she walked! God bless
us, she was a bad sight! She was like one of these disabled
children. She had her head down and her toes turned in. I
kept having to tell her, "Turn out your toes! Put up your
head! Get out your chest!" And I'd give her a kick when
we'd be walking along.

And she knew nothing, Sharon. The nuns never told them
nothing. She was sixteen but she only had a twelve- or an
eleven-year-old brain. I'd have to catch Sally by the arm and
make her listen to me. You know the way you get your
period every month, the way you buy pads and everything.
Sally didn't know nothing about that. She didn't know what
a bra was. But when I'd go to tell her, she'd say, "Go away,
you're not me mother!" And she'd make a bolt for her aunt
Maggie's.

I had to come out very broad with Sally, telling her about
the differ of boys and girls. "Oh, that fella's lovely," she'd
say.

"Come here till I tell you about that fella," I'd say. I had
to slap it into her face, telling her, "Don't let a man put his
hands in between your legs or don't let him kiss you—keep
your mouth closed. Close your lips if you don't like him."
Well, the poor girl nearly went mad with the shock, and
then Mick started going on bad.

We weren't long in the rooms when he give up his job at the brewery. He was about a month without work and we were drawing off the assistance. But then he got a job on the buildings; the assistance gave him a card to go to this job. He worked six months there, but he began to complain with his chest and then he wasn't able for the buildings no more.

Even when Mick was working, he was going on bad. He wouldn't give me any money to hand. I'd do the shopping on the weekends, and he'd go with me. I used to feel terrible in the shops, Sharon. Instead of me pickin' something, he'd pick it. And he'd pick the cheapest rubbish in the shop to save money for the pubs. I used to love to get a bit of cake and jam, something that the children would love, but he wouldn't let me. Sometimes I'd risk it and say to the servants [sales clerks] when they'd come over to serve us, "Well, I'll have that and that . . ." Later, I'd get kilt over it. Mick'd give me a couple of digs when he'd get home. But he was very good to himself. He'd get a whole load of meat and vegetables for himself. He rationed it, he'd put up his own nice bit of meat and he'd say, "Now don't touch that."

One day Mick left up his rations—a nice steak—and the poor kids were watching this piece of steak. So I decided I'd give it to them. "I'll give it to yous," I said. "He can't kill me for that." But that night in Mick comes, drunk.

"I want me supper," he roared, "Where's me steak?" Well, I started to tremble but I couldn't get out of the room because Mick always stood in front of the door.

"Wait till you hear what happened, Mick! The cat dragged it on the floor," I lied. We had a big cat belonging to us. Well, if you heard the swearin' out of Mick. He started lookin' for the cat, and he was running to kill the cat with the knife. Sally started screaming, she was only after coming back to us out of the convent.

"If I get the cat, I'll kill it," Mick was yelling. One of the neighbors then, this Indian man, came over.

"What's wrong? What's wrong?" he said. "You Irishes are

always going mad." And he started giving out about the Irish. "Oh, it's you, Mick, beating up on your wife again. I won't have this," he said. "I'm going to have the law." I could see Mick's face turning, so I ran to save the Indian man. I jumped in front of him, and Mick just run the knife right into me stomach. Out goes me. And the screams of Sally.

The law came then, and I was carried to Dudley Road Hospital. But I wouldn't go against Mick, I wouldn't have him charged. I said that he was drunk and I blamed meself. I said we started quarreling and that I fell some way on top of the knife. I was afraid to charge Mick in case the children would be sent away. Back in Ireland, they'd send your children to a reformatory and you'd never get them back. And I knew if I charged Mick, he'd kill me when he got out. None of the Travelling women charged their husbands for fear. Mick could have gettin' two year, but he was let out on probation.

Well, Sally was sick of Mick beating me up, so she went to live with me sister Maggie over in another part of Birmingham. And the next time, Mick destroyed me. I couldn't scream, he gave me that bad of a beating. It was over food again. I'd lost me allowance book and I was waiting a long time to get me new one and all this back money. In England that time, the allowance was good; in Ireland, you wouldn't get much. Well, on came me book this day with the check in it. Mick got it at the door and he said, "Come on down to the post office." So I went with him and I gave him all this money for the length me book was gone. I gave it to him out of fear.

We went off to the shops then, and Mick bought a little food and put the rest of the money in his pocket and started walking down to the pub to get drunk. I followed him down the street and into the pub and then me nerves went. "You're drinking me money! It's me family allowance he's drinking," I roared. I screamed him right out of the pub and made a show of him. The woman in the pub wouldn't serve him then. "Get out!" she said. "You should be ashamed of yourself."

Mick went on to another pub then. But when he got home that night, he locked the door, and he gave me the worst beating. The Indians tried to break the door down, but Mick told them to mind their own business. Mick went on to work in the day, but I was afraid to go to the law and I was that bad I couldn't get out of the bed.

One morning a man came to the door for the television because we hadn't paid our bills. And here I was in bed, and I said to him, "I'm dying." And I told him to go get the woman next door. Mick had her threatened, but in she comes anyway. She was an awful nice Irish woman. She was separated from her husband: he went away and left her with three kids to rear on her own. She'd help me if I was short, and I'd help her. When she saw me, she got the police and they took me to the Dudley Road Hospital again with injuries to me head and me chest. The police charged Mick and he got six months in prison—Winston Green. I got a lovely life while Mick was gone. The welfare came every week. They got me clothes. They did everything. And I went to Bush House and put me name in for a council house. And when Mick got out, he was bound never to hit me for three years.

There was only two Irish families living in this house, Sharon. The rest was Indians and Jamaicers. There must have been about ten families living there, all using the one kitchen. Well, some people say that pigs sleep in the kitchens of Irish houses. That's what they tell you in England. But I never seen the likes of this kitchen before. And there used to be war over the cooker. I'd be rushing to get Mick's dinner, a Jamaicer woman would be rushing to get her husband's dinner, a Indian woman would be cooking, and we'd all want the one dinner at the one time. And then we all had children coming home from school. We used to be in an uproar.

Mick understood well how hard it was, but he'd hammer me just the same when his dinner wouldn't be ready. I used to be trembling to get Mick's dinner made. And I was afeard of all the colored people. There was only two white families in the house, and we'd be eaten if we complained or only said anything—I heard that the Indians would put a knife into you. The Jamaicers was different. They was very nice people, very kind and easy to get on with. If they seen you a bit sick, they'd try to help you anyway they could. But the Indians wasn't a bit nice—the Indian women. Even if you were real civil to them and asked them anything, they'd snap at you. And they'd keep muttering their Indian language—you couldn't understand them.

I was in the kitchen one day—we were all trying to cook our dinners—and there was this big old Indian woman. She was an awful heavy woman, about fifteen stone [195 lbs.], with arms that would make my body altogether. She could box like a man, and the wicked look she used to give you would make you nervous. All the young Indian women were afraid of her. I was afraid of her too and I was very cowardly around her. If she told me to take off me kettle or saucepan, I'd take it up off the stove and be glad to get out of her way. But this day I was peeling potatoes and I didn't hear her. She was giving out, giving out, and I couldn't understand her. I thought all the Indian women were talking between themselves. But wasn't she giving out hell about me because me saucepan with me vegetables was on the cooker. She was already after pointing and giving out to me to take up me things. I'd already taken up one of me saucepans. Now, that left three rings. So I'd gone back to peeling again and didn't pay any mind to her.

But the next thing, didn't she come over and such a box she gave me—it nearly dropped me. Straight into me ear.

The pain in me ear and jaw was terrible. I turned around. She thought that I was going to run away because I always used to get out of her way. But I turned around quick, and I run me knife right through her.

I never meant it. I never meant to do it. It was the temper. I'd never attack anyone with a knife and I couldn't believe what happened meself. I stabbed her twice with the knife and the blood. . . . If you seen the blood and heard the roars of the Indian women as they ran for the law. I was shocked. I didn't run, I just stood there and I never even let go of the knife. I kept the knife in me hand. The next thing, I see's these two big police ladies coming in. In England, if it's a women that does anything, there's policewomen that comes for you. They're all trained to break your arms, and I knew if they got me I was finished. So I got against the sink and wouldn't move. And I wouldn't give them the knife. I told them I'd do the same to them, so's they wouldn't come at me. But they rushed in on me anyhow. One of them near broke me back the way she twisted me hands behind me. The other one had no bother just to throw me into the police car. I'm done with, I said to meself.

Then I started thinking of the children coming home from school, and I got frightened to death. Sally was working in the factory just down below me. So I told the police lady, "My children is coming home from school and them Indian women might get them. Will you drive to that factory and go in and tell me daughter to look after them." So they did. They were kind enough.

Now, I thought, when they get me down to the police station, they're going to lock me up and give me a good beating. But they didn't. They just brought me in and started writing down everything I'd done. The Indian woman was gone to hospital and she charged me. Then they left me a long time sitting in the barracks. The next thing, on comes a police lady and gives me a cigarette, "Have a smoke while you're waiting."

"What are you going to do with me? Are you letting me home or are you locking me up? I want to know." But she wouldn't tell me. "Oh, we'll see to you."

The next time, they came in with a lovely cup of tea and a sandwich and were ever so nice. They were really too nice to me. And I started thinking, they're very civil to me after what I'm doing. They must be going to put me in jail for a long time. But it was late in the day and I knew there was going to be no court that day, so I thought they'd lock me up and have me for court in the morning. And me heart was breaking with the worry of the kids. But the next thing they called me into another room. And when I went in, there was about six men sitting around in chairs, and there was one chair in the middle of the floor for me. When I seen this, I said to meself, maybe the woman is dead. And I started trembling.

"Don't be one bit scared," one man said.

"Why did you do it?" said another one. I told him I didn't remember doing it, that the woman got on my nerves. Then I showed him my face. That's what saved me. Me jaw turned all black and blue and when they seen the mark, they knew it was her fault. Then another fellow asked me why I did it, and then another. They kept asking me real quick. One would ask a question and then another and I had to answer them all. I started getting mixed up. Finally, I wouldn't answer them. I got that fed up, that I lost me temper and I screamed out. And what were some of them, only doctors. Only I didn't know it.

"It's all right now," one man said. "We won't ask you any more. We're finished with you. You'll be going home soon."

"Ah," said I to meself, "thank God I'll get back to the house." But when they opened the door to take me out, I seen a black van. It was all painted black, like the vans going in and out of the Bridewell in Dublin. When I seen this black yoke and the police lady opening the doors in the back, I nearly took me own life. "What are you putting me in that for?" I roared.

"We're taking you for a ride."

"I can't be going to jail. I'm not tried yet."

"No," they said, "you'll find out soon."

There was two more police ladies sitting inside and they put me in the middle. I don't know how long we were driving. I kept asking them where we were going but they wouldn't give me any information. They were laughing to one another. The next thing, we passed this big building with walls like a jail around it.

"Is this the jail?" I said.

"No, this is a hospital. This is where you're going. You're only going in here to be built up—you're run down."

And that's how I landed in the mental.

Nan was admitted to Highcroft psychiatric hospital on August 9, 1966. According to hospital records, she had threatened suicide at the police station and was diagnosed as suffering from "depression." At 104 pounds, she was also underweight and undernourished. Her teeth—those that had not fallen out or been knocked out—were in terrible condition. Her chest was bad: by this time, Nan had chronic bronchitis. She also had a drinking problem, although she never spoke of it, and looked far older than her forty-six years. Nan was placed in Elizabeth ward with thirty-five other women for a week's observation and rest. This is what the record states, but Nan's memory recorded other things.

THEY BROUGHT me first to where the real bad cases were. You'd see these women talking to themselves and picking up papers and eating them. Oh, I was frightened. And some of them were in a padded cell away to themselves. I couldn't see them, but I could hear the screams. God, it

scared me. Then they took me to the good part, the good
ward.

One morning they brought me off across the yard into a
big room with doctors and nurses. There was all these
machines and a chair made like a dental chair. I got back
into this and they strapped me in. Then they put these
things down over me head. When I come back, I couldn't
even think who I was or where I was. I never thought I had
children. Me whole memory went.

Coming back, it was like clouds, all clouds, and I was
trying to think, think. It was very annoying. It was scary with
all these white beds and all. The nurse was there over me
the whole time until I come really back to meself.

The second time was worse because I knew the way I was
going to feel. But thank God, that was the last time.

They were good to me in the mental. They gave me
everything to eat. They were even giving me teeth—the
nurses and doctors all wanted me to get in me teeth—but I
wouldn't hear tell of having false teeth. Then they wanted to
do me hair, get me hair permed. All free. And they had
dances for the patients. For the laugh of it, I went. And then
there was a big room for looking at television and a place
where you could play cards or games. It was a lovely place.

Still, I was worried about the kids. One day I was sitting
very miserable, in very bad humor, when a cigarette craving
came over me. I was run out of cigarettes and I had no
money. Then this nice nurse, an Irish nurse, said, "You look
very down on yourself. What's wrong with you?"

"Nurse," I said, "I'm in a very bad way. I have no money
and I'd love a cigarette."

"You should have told us," she said, "we'd have gotten
you cigarettes." And she gave me ten Silk Cuts that she had
under her apron. Well, I could have eaten the cigarettes she
gave me, I was so long with out them. "What part of Ireland
are you from?"

"I'm from Westmeath," I said.

"That's where I'm from." And when she got to talking to me, she knew me younger sister Angela and me mother and father. Another Irish nurse, a Kerry one, came up to me then.

"What were you when you were in Ireland?" she said.

"I was a Traveller."

"I know her people," said the other nurse.

"Can you read fortunes?" said the Kerry nurse.

"I can."

"Well, I must get you to read mine."

"I will," I said. But I was soon being persecuted. Every cup of tea the nurses' would get, one of them would say, "Come here, missus, read this cup."

For me own luck, I wasn't long waiting when they broke the news, "You're going home tomorrow." The doctor said I was all right, just run down. I went in rough and ready from the kitchen with only a greasy apron on me, but you wouldn't know me coming out. The welfare took my size, and the nurses gave me some clothes—they knew I was only on assistance. Well, that cheered me up a bit.

The welfare lady came and took me out of the mental in her car and took me back to the Indian flat. Mick was in our room. They'd told him the day before that I'd be coming home, and he had the place lovely and there was plenty of food. I was back two days when I had to go to court to sign back me kids. The welfare had taken all the kids and put them in care. Only Kevin. Kevin thought he was going to be sent away for good, so he hid under the bed.

We lived in the Indian flat about three weeks till the welfare got us a house. I didn't see the Indian woman no more. I think she moved away. It was like heaven when I moved into me own house in Handsworth. It wasn't much, all the houses were falling down, but still it was me own. I lived there two year. Mick was all right for a while but then he started the same thing over again, going out with his sons drinking.

Mick wasn't right, Sharon. God forgive me, but he should have been shot. There's one thing, Sharon, I'll never tell but after that I took a black disgust to him. He was a very evil man.

Three days before Christmas, and do you know what he done? On he goes at about ten o'clock to draw his two weeks money: there wasn't another penny coming then till two weeks after Christmas. "I'll get in an awful load of food for Christmas," he said. "I'll get in a couple of drinks, but I'm not taking no drink now. We'll have a nice quiet Christmas. I won't be long."

"Thanks be to God," I said. We had everything planned, and I was thinking of the nice peaceable Christmas we was going to have. But what did Mick do? He went on to the Labour and never came back.

There wasn't a crust of bread in the house—no coal, no nothing. That night, no sign of Mick. I thought he must be drinking with Tommy, his son, and that he'd come back late in a taxi with the food. The next day, still no Mick. I nearly went mental—the screams of me up and down the house. Sally was with me. She'd come back from Maggie's and was only after having the flu, but she got up and went to ring the welfare. They got the police and found out that Mick was gone. The police went to his sons, and they said, "He's gone to Ireland." The welfare gave me some money then, about eight pound. It wasn't the full money, but they gave me what would keep me going. And they brought me a box of Christmas presents—toys, food, coal. I thought it was very good. We had a lovely peaceable Christmas then, better than when Mick was there.

I never could trust Mick. He was always planning. Christmas was the only time he could have gotten away because the welfare used to visit my home every week to see was he giving me the money for the children and to see that I had enough food in the house.

About six months after, Mick wrote to his sons and they

brought me the news. But I wouldn't answer his letters. I never answered him. And I told his sons if they came with another letter, there'd be trouble—that I was going to tell the law.

I lived there on me own then until I got me second house. They were knocking down all the old houses in Handsworth, so I got a lovely new house on Dawes Avenue in West Bromwich. Oh, it was beautiful. I had a lovely big tree in me front garden, with pink blossoms. And outside the door, we had a lovely big back garden. There was three bedrooms, a parlor, a kitchen, and a toilet outside and one upstairs with the bathroom separate. I was ever so happy.

While living in West Bromwich, three more of Nan's children returned home. Joe came back for a while after leaving St. Joseph's home in Salthill and serving in the British army. He was now in his early twenties and had been on his own for several years. John returned too. He had left the home in Salthill two years before, working in a bakery in Charlestown, county Mayo, and then taking a series of odd jobs in Dublin. He had kept in touch with Joe and now came over to join the family. Kathleen was discharged from Father Hudson's Home. She was twelve and like all Nan's children who had been institutionalized, she returned home awkward and shy and emotionally confused. But even the instability of Nan's life provided the glow of warmth around which her children could gather.

WE WERE about three year on our own, Sharon. The children were going to school, even Eddie. I had me house lovely and spotless. And John and Michael were working. I used to have the time of me life. But this day didn't I get a pain, so when I got the kids to school I went down to the clinic and I told the doctor. He gave me tablets and a bottle to build me up. "You needn't come up to see me again," he said, "we'll go to see you in the house."

That afternoon I was sitting down when a rap came on the door. I peeked out and I could see a case—you know the way a doctor carries a case. It's the doctor all right I said to meself and I rushed to the door and opened it. But who was it? He had a big crazy hat on him and when I looked out the door first, I couldn't see his face.

Well, it took me a minute to speak. Then I thought to shove him out the door, but he gave the door a bang in on top of me. Me heart thumped. The children wasn't home, and John and Michael was working. I'm finished, I thought. "Oh, come in and I'll get you a feed," I said to him. But when I got to the kitchen, the pan was falling out of me hand.

"Don't be so nervous," Mick said. "if you don't want that pan across your head." And I needn't tell you, Sharon, the names he started in calling me. "Go ahead and get the police," says he, "you're living here and look at the life you're having. But you're going back to Ireland now. You better come back, because if you don't, I'm going to kill you. I don't care if I do ten year, I want me children back." Then he said, "I've a lovely comfortable trailer in Dublin and I'm getting a house."

"What kind of a house?"

"It's a lovely little council house. What you always wanted, with a lovely garden," Mick said.

"It would be better to be back in Ireland. . . ."

Mick got around me Sharon when he mentioned the house. And I was thinking of Kathleen. The doctors in England said the air in Brimingham wasn't agreeing too good with her and that a change could do her good. And I was thinking of all children—Sam, Brendan, and Eddie—that they should have a father. So I went back with Mick. I don't know why I went back, I was always soft and foolish. Sometimes I think I'm not really sensible.

I walked out and left everything in the house, never even told me neighbour I was going. Michael was after buying me a new electric cooker—he worked for it in the factory. And I had a three-piece suite, lovely and new. I was paying the club man for half of it. Everything in the house was beautiful.

I told Mick to wait till I sold me things, but he wouldn't hear of it. He was trying to rush me because the law in England wanted him over his going off with the children's money at Christmas and he'd get jail if he was caught. John was living near his work in a flat then, but he came by when I was leaving. "John, you sell the things," I said. "Sell the stuff and keep the money. I'm going home to Ireland."

John sold some of me things, but what did my neighbour do? She locked me door, and when John got a buyer for the cooker, she said, "Your mother's gone and nobody is getting anything out of that house, not till I ring the Council." My John was always a bit nervous, so he went off and left the rest in the house. I suppose the Council threw it out.

And when I got back to Ireland, what did Mick have? Not even a tent.

X

Holylands

It was mid-morning when Nan and the children arrived in Ireland in July 1970. They had boarded the ferry in Liverpool the night before and slept sitting up, their suitcases and bags piled around them, on a ship crowded with summer visitors. They emerged, tired and bedraggled, and walked from the pier into the city for a meal of sausages and chips. Then they caught a bus for Coolock, a suburban village on the north side of Dublin. And now Mick was leading them down Belcamp Lane, a long narrow road surrounded by flat, open fields.

The air was dry, and their feet kicked up dust as they walked along the edge of the road. Ahead they could see dots of red and yellow clustered together in a corner of the field. Soon, trailers, wagons, and tents took shape, and piebald ponies materialized among the cows grazing on the rich grass.

Mick had been staying with Sally—who had moved to Dublin the previous year—and her new husband, Billy. Billy was a settled lad who had been thrown out of home by his father and had taken to the streets, mixing first with tramps, later with Travellers. At first, he had met secretly with his mother, but now that he had married Sally, all ties with his family were cut. He offered Nan a cigarette and seemed nice enough. Sally made tea, and they sat down to talk while the children ran off.

It wasn't long before Nan realized that Mick had nowhere

for them to stay. There had never been a trailer, and as she would discover, it would be a long time before she saw the inside of a house. As evening approached, she began complaining to anyone who could hear and ended up swapping the small silver watch she had pinned to her sweater—the only valuable object she had—to another Traveller, plus ten pounds, for a large canvas tent cover.

The next morning she asked Billy to write to John, and in two weeks John and Michael arrived. They pooled what money they had with Mick to buy a pony and cart and began foraging for scrap metal and for lumber to build two shacks—one for Nan, Mick, and the kids and another for themselves. They scavenged through the mountains of garbage in Ringsend and combed the neighborhoods for the rest. At a convent not far from camp, they were given three horse-hair mattresses and metal beds.

Soon Nan was laboring to turn her "hut" into a home—sewing curtains, papering the walls, and laying pieces of carpet on the floor. The boys installed a woodstove and built a fence between the shacks, so Nan could plant flowers in a protected place. And when Michael returned from scrap collecting one day with a statue of Our Lady, missing one hand, Nan took it as a good omen and set about gathering stones and rooting up bluebells and snowdrop bulbs in the woods nearby to build a little rockery around it. The end result of all this work was "lovely and comfortable"; and the winter passed uneventfully, except for quarrels with Mick. And a broken jaw.

The following spring, a social worker and a nun from the south side of the city visited the families. A school for Travelling children had been set up at the convent in Miltown, and a temporary camping site for "itinerant" families—as the government and news media now referred to them—had been opened in nearby Rathfarnham. They encouraged Nan to move and place her children in school. She was assured that the local itinerant settlement committee—one of the numerous volunteer citizens' groups which were organizing around the country to help Travellers—would provide her with a trailer at nominal rent. A minibus would collect the children and take them to school. It was too good to refuse.

I met Nan a few weeks after she had moved to "Holylands," as the site was called. It was little more than a plot of land sandwiched between a housing estate and the playing fields of the neighborhood school.[27] Here about twenty families parked their trailers and wagons on two wide asphalt strips located at either end of a small central field; their only amenity was a water tap. The site was surrounded by trees and looked into the Dublin Mountains, giving it a rural air despite piles of scrap metal and garbage accumulating in the ditches and in back of a wall behind the trailers.

Three large, extended families lived in Holylands: the Donohoes, Connors, and Maughams. But the site's population was in constant flux as individual households came and went, and relatives arrived for visits. Nan's immediate family at the time included Mick, six sons—John, Michael, Kevin, Sam, Brendan, and Eddie—and Kathleen. Later James, his wife, Mary, and their seven young children moved on, as did Sally and Billy and their new baby. Three of Mick's brothers also lived at Holylands for a while. A niece of Nan's and her family of nine spent the winter. Nan's daughter Eileen, whom she hadn't seen since she had taken that last lingering look through the window of the hospital nursery in Mullingar seventeen years before, appeared like a phantom from the past and stayed for two weeks. And so did Willie, after slaving for a Galway farmer for four years upon his release from St. Joseph's in Salthill. The farmer had promised him some land in time— that was why he'd given Willie no wages—but after four years Willie wisely gave up.

Nan and Mick were related to both of the other families in camp. Mick's first wife had been a sister of Old Jim, the patriarch of the Connors clan. Nan was a "far-out friend" to Nanny Nevin, the matriarch of the Maughams. For the most part, however, the Donohoes, Connors, and Maughams each kept to themselves, camping in their own area of the site and independently carrying out their daily round of business and social activities. But in times of serious trouble and need, they helped each other out with food and small loans and occasionally, they formed temporary work alliances. And once, with the coaching of a lay religious worker, young men and boys from all three families formed the Wagon Wheels soccer team.

I began living in Holylands with my husband, George, in the summer of 1971, after six weeks of almost daily visits. Nan and Mick and several other Travellers had suggested we move into camp in order to stop paying rent for a flat, and we wanted nothing better than to live with Travellers. So with Mick Donohoe's help, we purchased a barrel-top wagon from a Traveller across the city and a mare from Paddy Maugham.

We parked our somewhat dilapidated wagon between Nan's trailer and that of Red Mick and Katie Connors, who later became our good friends, and set about refurbishing it. As George repaired a broken window frame above the front door, Mick built a second one for us from new wood, carving it to match. Without asking or being asked, Michael and John repainted the undercarriage canary yellow and the body a brilliant red—the "real" Traveller colors, everyone assured us—carefully avoiding the hand-painted horse heads, fruit clusters, and elaborate scroll work that covered the door and side panels. Nan came over one morning with a "lucky" horse shoe for our door. Paddy Maugham generously gave us a pair of shafts, and his son Anthony helped look after our horse. Nanny Nevin offered advice on new floor tiles and curtains. Young girls asked how long we would stay and tightened their eyebrows skeptically when I said "a year." And so we merged into the traffic of camp routine.

Days started with the whir of the electric van that delivered pints of milk to families with young children, as part of the government's free milk scheme. Not long after, men and women began to emerge from their trailers and shacks to splash cold water on their faces and issue orders for the kettle to be filled. Someone would then stoke the campfire or pump the primus. While teenage sons ran to the fields above the site to check on the horses, the men sat down on tree stumps and broken chairs to wait for their tea. The women sliced slabs of bread and coated them with butter, occasionally jiggling the rashers and eggs sizzling in a blackened pan. At ten o'clock, the school minibus arrived to pick up the children who milled around the watchman's hut, giggling and shouting. Nan's only children in school were Sam and Brendan who had already set off on foot for the local Christian Brothers' school. After attending school in England, they were too advanced for the convent's Traveller school.

By eleven, most men and older boys had climbed into their lorries or hitched up their mares to begin gathering scrap. Michael usually went with his brother John, but for a while he worked with his step-brother, James. Later in the year, he found a job with a cleaning firm, but quit after only a few weeks. The strain of getting up early, working long hours, hiding his Traveller identity, and putting up with ridicule from some of the younger men in camp proved too much. John avoided similar problems when he got a job in a garage by moving to a cheap bedsitter in the city.

Shortly after the men left, a caravan of toddlers, women, and prams wound its way down the lane. Most women walked from door to door in the suburbs, but some begged the "streets"—a lower-status activity. They sat on O'Connell Bridge wrapped in a plaid "rug" with a baby in their lap and a cardboard box at their feet or else paced back and forth in front of busy stores, accosting passers-by for a "copper" or "a bit of help," while keeping a wary eye out for the police. Nan's daughter-in-law Mary usually sat on the Haypenny Bridge or behind Trinity College at a place "where three buses meet." Nan never allowed Kathleen to beg on the streets, although I know she occasionally did.

When a relative was scheduled to appear in court, family

ABOVE. America, CO. Mayo, at the turn of the century. Nan encountered many scenes like this while peddling in the West. *(Lawrence Collection, National Library of Ireland)* LEFT. Travellers moving to a new camp pass through the town of Cashel. *(Pat Langan)*

ABOVE. Travelling families on the road to Dublin. *(Pat Langan)*
LEFT. A muddy urban camp in the early 1970s. *(Pat Langan)*

ABOVE. A Traveller girl sits inside her family's winter shelter, a humble but comfortable shack made from scrap timber scavenged at the dump. *(George Gmelch)*

RIGHT. A Holylands girl and her younger sister beg on O'Connell Bridge in the heart of Dublin. *(Pat Langan)*

ABOVE. Michael Donohoe washes a mare near Blessington, CO. Wicklow. *(George Gmelch)*
LEFT. Nan cooks breakfast outside her trailer at Holylands. *(George Gmelch)*

ABOVE. Family life at Holylands. *(George Gmelch)*
RIGHT. Nan hangs her laundry on lines strung in the
field behind her trailer.
Most Travellers simply
spread their laundry on the
bushes to dry. *(Pat Langan)*

Sally Donohoe bathes her infant in a makeshift tub at Holylands. *(George Gmelch)*

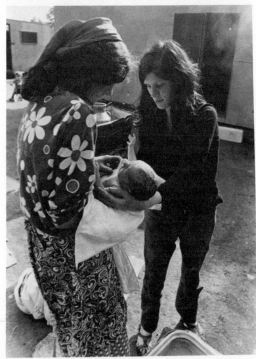

Nan and Sally at Holylands. *(Pat Langan)*

ABOVE. Mick (center), Nan and Old Jim Connors at a pub in the Dublin Mountains. *(Pat Langan)*

BELOW. Reconciled in their last years together, Nan and Mick enjoy a quiet pint with their granddaughter Nanzer. *(George Gmelch)*

Nan. *(Pat Langan)*

members rushed to the courthouse to watch. Travelling men were often fined for wandering horses, overdue motor tax, or drunk driving; occasionally, someone was charged with theft or assault.

While the working adults were away, Holylands was peaceful: a few old men sitting around, a few women cleaning their trailers or sweeping the ground. A social worker or nun might visit, but otherwise the only sounds were quiet voices, the clatter of domestic chores, and an occasional barking dog.

At three o'clock children raced screaming from the school minibus, greyhounds and lurchers snapping at their heels. Speeding lorries screeched to a halt, cab doors slammed, and men walked to the campfires to talk and joke. Women nudged bulging prams up the rutted lane and then busied themselves with dinner, bribing one child to the shops with a few extra bob for sweets and shouting orders to the others: "MYLEE . . . COME HOME . . . Come home, Mylee, or I'll break your face!" Occasionally, a police car rolled in and a crowd formed to watch as the *shades* asked questions, and the Traveller they were talking to answered cooperatively, revealing nothing.

Nan rarely left the site. At fifty-two, she felt too old and weak to beg. She'd never liked it much anyway, not the way many Travelling women did. For them begging was a relief from camp routine, an opportunity to match wits with housewives and learn how settled people lived. They also relied on it to provide for much of their family's daily needs, and had polished hard-luck stories and ingratiating ways. The most successful women developed "ladies" or patronesses who regularly gave them food and money as well as sympathy and advice. And sometimes they could even take a bath.

But Nan didn't beg and partly because she didn't, the Donohoes were one of the poorest families in camp. Kathleen, who was thirteen, had never begged before and was a bit young for her age. Nan frequently complained about her playing with dolls, while other girls like Maggie Connors, who was also thirteen, were "clever" and "bold" and already being considered for marriage. Twelve-year-old Sam and ten-year-old Brendan were much more skilled at begging, although Sam often used it as a pretext to sneak away and learn Karate. (Today he is a blackbelt.) Even Eddie, who was eight, was sometimes successful. Kevin stayed in bed as much as he could and like many teenage boys only went out to beg when he wanted the "price of the pictures" [movies] and fags. Nevertheless, each child usually managed to bring Nan a few bob and a loaf of bread, a tin of beans, or a quarter of tea. She never thanked them; they were expected to help. Nan even got angry one day when Sam brought home three pounds, but revealed that he had gotten it by telling people his mother was dying in hospital. She was less upset with the lie, than the possibility it might come true.

Michael and John contributed substantially to the family income, giving Nan a portion of their weekly dole or wages as well as part of the proceeds from any sale of scrap. They helped her fix up her trailer, and when their sister Eileen and new husband planned a visit, they chipped in to buy new sheets, cups, and plates. But when Eileen arrived, she scandalized them by wearing red "hot pants." The men in camp joked from a distance, but the women came by to stare.

"Ah, look at your chubby legs, God bless you!" Nanny Nevin said to skinny Eileen.

"Just because Travellers don't like anyone who doesn't wear a long heavy skirt ... I'd trust a person who wears different clothes more, they're more honest," Nan said in a rushed and confused defense. "What are Travelling girls hiding?" But she didn't like it either.

Mick gave Nan four or five pounds each week for food, less than what many men gave. He also collected some scrap and during the summer, combed the neighborhoods for knives and lawnmowers to sharpen. But much of the year he was incapacitated by drink and ill health. Nevertheless, Mick was vain and rubbed black shoe polish in his hair to cover the gray. He kept his shoes polished too and always wore suits.

Michael and John called him Al Capone because of his slicked-back hair and wide lapels. "You mightn't believe it," Mick told me once, after describing what a beauty Nan had been, "but I wasn't bad-looking meself." He then pointed to the scars that marred his face and pushed and pulled at his jowls to show me how they had changed shape.

On warm evenings, everyone sat at the campfires talking. Sometimes a group gathered and tales from the road were told: of horses balking at a haunted bridge, of being mysteriously lost in an open field, of trickery and clever deals, of treachery and narrow escapes. Mick was a good story-teller and had many adventures to narrate. We all listened quietly in the dark, drinking our tea, as tree limbs creaked overhead and the flames danced. A spark would fly or the smoke shift and a bad omen would be read or luck foretold. When there were only a few at the fire, I often asked about the old days of travel and country life. And if only women were around, we talked about the mischief of men, the evils of the city, and the boldness of children. When Nan and I were alone, this often led to stories of her family and personal accounts.

NOBODY KNOWS that happened to me brother John—did I ever tell you that, Sharon? He was killed in the North, but we never knew who killed him. He used to go into Belfast to a pub in Smithfield. And they all knew him well; they used to call him "Big John Donohoe." He was a big blondy-haired man, the biggest of all me brothers. But anyhow, he probably got a few bottles and when he got drunk, he got on his bike and made home. The barman bid him good night. But that was the last John was seen alive. He was found bleeding to death on the path, going up the Falls Road. The guards picked him up and put him in a cell and locked him up. They thought because he was drunk, he wasn't much hurted.

The next morning they were out looking for his wife and

family to say he was dead. His wife was in hospital waiting
to have her baby, and they couldn't tell her. So they brought
him into the morgue and had an inquest. The head was
split; it was like he got an awful belt of something very
sharp. The guards said that they didn't know. But they
should have been getting an ambulance, Sharon, he was
covered in blood. But they threw him into a cell instead, just
like a dog and let him die. They could have saved his life or
they could have gotten him time. But they got him dead
instead.

Young adults and teenagers often departed to see a film,
usually a Western, which they later told in meticulous detail.
They dressed up to go—a few of the women owned fur coats—
and went alone or in small groups of three or four to make
it easier to get in, since not every cinema's management
admitted Travellers. When there was a television in camp and
the lorry wasn't needed for the pictures or pub, it was backed
up to the trailer and cables attached to the battery and fed
through the window. Then the campfires emptied of everyone except the old, and the trailer filled to capacity with
spellbound faces watching advertisements as intently as the
programming. My own perceptions of Traveller life were often
sharpened. Like the time someone momentarily switched to
a symphony and Katie Connors couldn't understand why the
musicians were playing at once; for Travellers, the individual
singer or melodian player is key. Or the advertisement for
"Stork" margarine that elicited the remark that "only *buffers*
[non-Travellers] eat margarine" and the information that Dublin
Travellers for a while referred to settled people derisively as
"storks" and "margarine eaters." Or the important clues Travellers missed in dramas and detective films because of some
subtlety of language or a printed sign which no one had read.
It was then I reminded of what a handicap illiteracy is.
    When the weather was fine, life took place outdoors. But

dark dreary days and wet, bone-chilling nights outnumbered the dry. Then it was too damp or cold for the women and children to go begging or the men to collect scrap, and people stayed home. Campfires lay smoldering or dead. Days and nights were spent crowded inside stuffy trailers with no relief from the demands of children and no escape from the intrusive visits of neighbors who would enter boldly to borrow a broom or stand silently in the shadows listening for gossip and news. When this happened, private conversations, like chameleons changing color, imperceptibly transformed themselves into trivial chat or some well-known fact—pierced ears improve your sight, food in the city is bad.

Some nights a child ran past the trailers yelling "The Legion's here!" at which the adults fell silent or groaned, quickly blew out their candles and moved away from the door. "The Legion's here" meant members of the local chapter of the Legion of Mary—a Catholic lay group—had arrived in camp to visit the families and cajole them into saying the Rosary.

When they came up to a trailer and peered in, they were usually ignored. Except by Nan, who always felt sorry for them and went over to talk. But sometimes the Legion simply barged in, and when they did, the men automatically got up and walked out, forcing their wives to listen while they were rebuked like little children for not attending Mass. The women often reversed roles, taking the opportunity to complain about their health, their poor trailers, the social worker not doing her job, their children still not being able to read or write, the Corporation, and anything else that came to mind.

Once, Nan complained about Eddie's confirmation being delayed a second time. And seeing what she perceived to be a chance to proselytize, the woman responded, "Mrs. Donohoe, I think it's because the nuns see that you and Mr. Donohoe never go to Mass that they're keeping Eddie back. Because what's the use of his first communion, if his parents are setting a bad example."

"Eddie'll never make his first communion then, because I

give it up," Nan stated. But before she could say anything else, the woman pulled a colored picture of Christ's crucifixion from her pocket and held it before Nan.

"Look at Jesus' face. Isn't he sad?" she said.

"Yeah, he looks sad," Nan sighed.

"Jesus is hurt when his children don't go to Mass."

"I say me prayers to meself when I feel like it," Nan responded. "Anyway, it's not fair to punish children for their parents' mistakes."

"You're right," she conceded, leaving soon after.

It was at times like this that the warmth, temporary cheer, and chosen companionship of the pubs beckoned. Not every publican would serve Travellers, however, especially when they arrived in groups. But when one who did was found, the camp emptied of young couples and men who spent their evenings, and most of their savings, drinking and playing "pontoons" and "twenty-one." While the men joked and performed tricks with matches, the women talked, disappearing into the ladies room to swap clothes or boots. Later in the evening, someone would use the pay phone to call the hospital to check on a sick child; gastroenteritis and bronchitis were serious problems, expecially in winter. The mother or father would then return to the table and duplicate the nurse's words in a mechanical and slightly bewildered way: "His condition is considerably improved. He's resting comfortably."

For many, the unspoken goal of a visit to the pub seemed to be to drink as much as possible in the time allotted, with men calling round after round and rushing to the bar at closing time to place a final order. It was customary to finish the evening seated around a table packed with black pints of Guinness and untouched glasses of gin and orange.

At home, marital grievances rose to the surface on a river of drink and swelled into noisy arguments. Wives who had sat in their trailers all evening were angry at being left behind; those who had gone to the pub were upset with their husband's extravagant spending. Travelling men were "jealous" and watched their wives carefully. And later, even a harmless act, like offering a cigarette to another man, could be used as an excuse to start a fight. Then the camp would wake to the sounds of crashing crockery and shattering glass, ear-piercing screams and guttural curses. Thursday nights were always the worst; it was the day the men collected the dole. "It's a terrible life," Nan remarked to me one Friday, "when you sit around waiting for it to get dark so you can go to bed and then you can't even sleep because of the fighting and noise."

The next day amid the debris of broken dishes and stale food, new arguments would erupt. Hangovers made it hard to work and reinforced the need to drink. And before anyone realized it, a binge had begun. To continue it, wedding rings were hocked, horses sold, and expensive trailers swapped for decrepit ones plus cash. Other families perched above the carnage like friendly birds of prey waiting to drop in, extend credit, and carry off wagons, radios, and more.

Wives sometimes fled to their parents' camp, leaving the older children behind for their husbands to care for. After a couple weeks, the men were eager to bring them back and took pledges before a priest not to drink for six months, a year, or even a "lifetime." Nan went to England and stayed with her sister Maggie for two weeks the year I was in Holylands to escape three weeks of Mick's drunken arguing and abuse. To maintain his binge, Mick sold his pony and cart—and with it, Michael and John's livelihood—and spent £95 on drink.

Less often, a man left home to spend a few days downtown in the Iveagh Hostel or to travel to England for work. Sometimes, the end came with a lorry accident and injuries. Then there was little choice but to stop drinking and begin the slow upward climb toward wealth and respectability again.

My first night in camp was a Thursday in early September. The evening started quietly; I sat at the campfire talking to Nan, while George visited Granny and Jim Connors at the top of the site. We both returned around ten, eager to enjoy the novelty and comfort of our snug wagon. I climbed into bed, jotted down notes from the evening's conversation, and then opened a book. About an hour later, several lorries sped into camp. The squeal of tires and brakes alarmed me, until I realized that it was just the men returning from the pubs. I continued reading, lying securely under the ribcage of the felt-lined canvas roof. And soon the patches of loud talking faded, and I blew out the lamp and fell asleep.

At four in the morning I awoke. A woman had screamed just outside the wagon. I sat up and listened. There were more screams, then a thud and the sound of splintering glass, followed by running footsteps on the pavement. I leaped out of bed, stepped to the door and parted the curtains, straining to see. George stayed in bed. There wouldn't have been enough room for two of us at the window, and the wagon roof was just low enough that he could never stand up straight. There were more screams, followed by a slam and a male voice yelling, "Come out, you whore! Open this door . . . you and your cowardly mongrels!" The door must have come open because a woman's voice shrieked, "Kill him, boys!" There was scuffling and a few minutes later, the man called out in a trembling and vulnerable voice, "Look at that, Nan. Look at me face. They cut me face."

I stood at the door for perhaps a half hour more, then got back into bed. But I had trouble falling asleep. I had never been so close to violence before. The next day, the Donohoes sat subdued and sheepish at their campfire. And the other Travellers gave them disapproving looks as they walked by and coyly asked George and me how well we'd slept.

During the year that followed, Nan frequently complained to me about her trailer door. The lock was bad, and the door opened out rather than in and therefore couldn't be barricaded. At first, such comments surprised me, but later merely dismayed me as I began to realize just how strategically she had to think.

This was the pace of Traveller life—weeks of pleasant, if

not boring, routine puntuated by drama and marital crisis, usually brought on by drink.

Most of Nan's days were spent washing clothes in a steel tub and spreading them on the bushes to dry, fixing up her trailer, badgering Sam and Brendan to stay in school, encouraging Michael to get a job and fending off his wedding plans. But she was also involved in thirteen fights that year. Once she was hit on the back of the head with a Guinness bottle; she lost three teeth when she hit the floor. Once when both she and Mick were drinking, Nan in desperation pulled open my wagon door and ended up climbing into my bed to hide, while George went outside to stand and make his presence known. When Mick staggered to the door and asked if I'd seen Nan, I sat up tall and said she wasn't there.

I left Holylands in August 1972. Two months later, Nan sold her trailer, moved into a barrel-top wagon, and left the site. When I saw her again in the summer of 1975, I asked why.

I WAS getting browned off with Rathfarnham, and I couldn't get anybody to move me trailer. Nobody would oblige me. Everyone was busy and more of them had no tow bar. I didn't want to be under a compliment to them anyhow, Sharon. So I thought if I sold me trailer and bought a wagon, the boys could shove it out. A wagon was the handiest and quickest way out of the site.

Mick was staying in the Iveagh. But when he came back and saw me with a wagon, he bought one too. Then he went round the roads looking for a wall or a nice place to pull in. He come back one day and said, "I know where there's a lovely place we could stay for a few months. There's nobody down there, only Sally and Billy." So Mick got the lend of a horse off Paddy Maugham, and Paddy's son Anthony, the Lord have mercy on him, pult him down. Michael and John wheeled my wagon out and shoved it down the hills; the land was a whole fall down to where we were going. Then we pushed it in at the back of Patrick's Cottages on the Grange Road, Rathfarnham.

We weren't long there when Mick went into hospital for an operation. He stayed for about three weeks. It was cancer in the stomach, only I didn't know it. I talked to the doctor, but the doctor didn't give me any information. Mick was worried and didn't want the doctor to tell us. "It wasn't much," he said. "Something gathered in the bottom of me stomach. That's what caused me all the pain, the doctor said that when they'd cut that out, I'd be as right as ever." And Mick was real happy and he felt well for six months after, but then he begin to get the pains back and he started to drink again. But we didn't quarrel. I think now Mick was afraid of being left, of being alone.

We used to go to Rathfarnham and sit on the bank of this lovely little stream at the end of the village. We couldn't drink in camp because other Travellers had pulled in next to us, and the kids would be around us. So we'd go to the river for peacesake. One day Mick said, "Meet me down in Rathfarnham." And he went in to the labor. It was after raining real hard—three or four heavy rains—then it came to sunshine. So I walked to the village and met him, and we went into the off-license and got our bottles and went to the river and sat down. We had a few drops of whiskey and Guinness, and we were real happy, very contented just speaking away.

But what happened? Didn't the kids from the cottages on the other side of the river start tormenting us. They were making a laugh of us and trying to fire stones to get us away: "Get out of that! Get out of that, you old winers! Get away, you knackers! You won't drink there anymore."

"I'm going round to tell your mother," Mick give out to them.

"Ah, leave the children alone," I said. "If you don't look at them, they won't notice you. Turn your back to them, Mick."

But the children gave us no peace. We kept drinking anyway; we had nowhere else to go. But didn't the children get
on my nerves then. I got a rap of something on the back of
me neck. It didn't hurt me, but it annoyed me. And I was
drunk, only I didn't know I was. "I'll put yous going," I
roared, and didn't I make a run for them. I only meant to
run a little bit but down I went, right over the bank and into
the middle of the river. And the flow of the water after all
the rain. . . . I was like a butterfly on the top of the water. I
roared for Mick to save me.

"I can't. I can't," he said, and he was nearly falling in
trying to save me. "Hold on! Hold on," he said. "Hold on,
Nan." But how could I hold on to nothing? "You'll be all
right when you get to the bridge," Mick said.

Thank God there was trees growing along the bank and I
grabbed onto the trees. But if you heard the roars and
laughs of the children, Sharon: "The woman is drowned!
The old gypsy one is drowned!"

One of the men out of the settlement come out and
dragged me out of the river. "You're a very lucky woman,"
he said. I was soaked, and the laughs of them kids were terrible. But I never did a haypert [anything]. The day was
lovely and warm and I just took off me heavy things and left
them there and kept on the rest of me clothes. I looked like
a drowned rat.

"Come on," said Mick. "We'll go up there where they
can't torment us." So we went up near the road and sat on a
wall, and the clothes dried on me.

The next time we went to the river, the children took no
notice. They were used to us then. And we sat on the bank
drinking cider. Mick was fond of cider and he got us two
bottles and two baby Powers [whiskey]. We were talking real
sensible about what we were going to do. We were thinking
of getting the lend of a pony and moving to the other side
of the city. We were getting tired of the Grange Road; we'd
been too long in the one place.

It was getting late of a summer evening, and Mick was getting well drunk. The two of us were sitting there peaceable, speaking and staring up at the sky. But I got this feeling and I looked over me shoulder and I give a jump. There was a plain wooden cross hanging in the sky. Mick was talking about when we'd leave, but I wasn't answering him. I kept looking, looking at it.

"You bothered fool," Mick said, "what's wrong with you? You're not paying any heed. Don't you want to leave Rathfarnham?"

"No, it's not that Mick. Look up at the sky."

"What's wrong with the sky?" he said. "I see stars."

"Do you not see the wooden cross right frontinst you?" I said.

"You're mental," Mick said. "You're not right. I shouldn't go out with you at all." He stood up, "You're not getting no more of this now." Mick still had a lot of cider left.

"I swear. There it is," I said. The two of us started arguing then. We got real hot tempered. "I'm not a fool," I said. "I seen a cross."

"Go away," Mick said and he made a swipe at me.

"Go ahead and hit me," I said. "I hope something happens to you now because you don't believe me."

"You're getting no more of this drink," Mick said. 'You can see any cross you like." And he took up his bottle and went on. But I didn't care, I was worrying about the cross. I caught up to Mick at the Yellow House, the big pub in Rathfarnham.

"Hold on Mick. Wait a minute," I said.

"No," he said, "I'm not going in there."

"No, I don't want you to go into the Yellow House. I want you to come into the house of God for a minute," I said. There's a chapel just across the road.

"Now don't swear on a lie," he said.

"I won't," I said. And I went up to the altar and kneeled down and swore what I'd seen about the cross, just to make

Mick believe me. Then I said a few prayers. When I got finished, Mick was gone out of the chapel, making back for camp. When I got there, he was drinking.

That night Mick took a pain, and the doctor came and give him some stuff but the stuff was no good. "Get me a taxi," Mick said. The next day all the boys went in to see him in the hospital. "Your mother was right," he said. "I didn't believe her." And right over his head in the hospital was this same size of a wooden cross that I'd seen in the sky. "I must be going to die," he said.

"It's a funny thing, Sharon, but anytime I dream of a cross, there's always trouble." But that time, I did see it. It was no dream that time.

Mick had another operation then but whatever happened, he lost the power of his leg—the left leg—and his whole side down along, bar the hand. He was four months in hospital. I never seen a sadder thing than when Mick was dying. It was the longest I ever seen anybody dying—lingering, lingering, lingering.

Me, my John, Michael, all of us, waited around his bedside. We were in every day, waiting. It was sad to look at Mick, his poor eyes would turn up looking at you and he'd try to bring you over to him. Then he'd doze off asleep again. And then he'd waken and try to hold on to you. Mick grabbed me all the time, trying to keep hold of me. I was sneaking out one time, and he wakened and tried to grab me.

"Sit there now, you," he said. "You've time enough to go home. You wait here with me." He couldn't say it real plain; his voice would come and go.

"I just want to go home to look after the kids," I said.

"They're well able to mind themselves. Don't worry," he said. "Wait now with me." He wanted me to sit there all the time with him. "You'll get a place out of here," he said. And the last words he ever spoke plain were, "I wish I had the house." He knew I was all the time worrying about a house, praying for a house to get the children off the road.

His voice went altogether then. He couldn't speak for two weeks and at the last he was trying to tell me something. It was very important whatever it was, because he kept trying but I never did hear it. Mick was shaking, shaking. Then he fell asleep. The head nurse said, "He won't die till maybe sometime tomorrow. I think you can go home and get a rest." So we all went back to the flat where Sally'd moved and laid down.

Billy got up in the morning about nine and rang the hospital. He used to ring about Mick every day. He came back and said, "Mick died at seven o'clock this morning." Well, Sharon, I got so's I couldn't speak. I thought to speak, but my voice and all left me. And you know the way they all run, run, run to you.

Everyone came to see me—brothers' sons and all. But I didn't want to see anybody. And they all brought Guinness, whiskey, wine. Even James came with baby Powers. But I wouldn't touch a drop of it. Nobody could believe it, they thought I'd swallow all the drink I could to get it off me mind. But no. I never touched a drink for all that week, not till Mick was buried and I got back from the funeral.

I'm after going though an awful life, Sharon. "I don't know why I kept with Mick. Fair play to him, he was very kind to me first. If I only went to the well for a bucket of water, he'd go with me to carry it. And he could tell good stories—I'd rather Mick than any other man I met. And when the children was young, he used to make a fuss over them; although he didn't like the bother of looking after them. But when Mick'd get drunk, he was a different man. He'd get very contrary. I think when he was drunk, he thought about his life and he used to take it out on everybody.

Mick was never really happy. He told me several times he never really loved his first wife. That when he was young, he was going with some other girl—and he really did love this girl—but he got mixed in with some Travelling People and his wife was belonging to them. She was all the time after him, Mick said, and one night he got drunk and she met him and he went off with her and when he sobered up, he was afraid to go back because there was a big crowd of her people. So he kept going with her. But in the end, he turned back and brought her back to her father and married her. But Mick said he never really loved her. He told me several times. But I don't know, Sharon. Mick must have loved his first wife because when he'd get drunk, he'd be lamenting and crying over her. It often got on me nerves.

When I think of all I done for Mick and of all the cruelty, I couldn't really have been sensible. No other woman would have done what I done for him. I used to go out and sell, I'd get his pony and yoke it, I'd get the fire—I'd do the man's work and the woman's work—and every penny I'd get, I'd hand it up to him. If I didn't, I'd know what would be at the end of it—a beating. I kept him clean—his shirts, his bed, everything was spotless. And I kept him well fed. I used to buy everything for him: meat, eggs, custard, jelly, apples. I fed him up like a baby. He always had plenty of pocket money and all. And the funny thing is, Mick was good at earning a living himself. He'd work with farmers or he'd work on the docks, he'd work here and there, but only for a month or two. But I'd have to do twelve months hard work.

I don't think Mick really loved me, he stayed because he had the best time that a man ever had. He only wanted me for a skivvy—you know, a slave. No matter what he'd tell me to do, I'd do it for him because I was soft and foolish. I was a great soft skivvy for him. Then when the family allowance came, Mick had that. The more children I'd have for him, the more money he'd get.

When I pray for Mick now sometimes I think, should I pray for him? Because Mick was a wicked man in the end. He was cruel to me and not only me, he broke many a person's heart. We wouldn't be no length in a place, when he'd try to do away with me. The doctor's paper at Dudley Road Hospital was that length about all the beatings I got in England. There's none of my body that's not marked—me legs, me face. If me hair was shaved, Sharon, you'd get a fret. I hate to rake me hair, the comb keeps falling into ridges. Mick broke me nose in Belfast—I forgot to tell you that. Me nose was over on the side of me face, and the doctors had to straighten it up. My God, I'm in bits. I don't know how I'm alive.

Still, I forgived him on account of the children. But I can't bear looking at his photos today, I'd rather take them and burn them. And I would, only I don't want to hurt the children's feelings or spoil their love.

I never got at the reason Mick was so cruel. I suppose he never thought about going out of this world. I suppose Mick thought he'd live for life.

After Mick was dying, the Corporation came and moved all the families, only me. Me house was coming up and they didn't want the bother of running round trying to find me. The other families got vexed. I'd be vexed meself, if I was moved but I seen one family left. But I explained to them. They were satisfied then, but still the odd one moved back after the Corporation was going. They wouldn't be there two days when the guards would come and move them off again. I begin to worry—what is the people thinking? That I'm giving information, that I'm a squealer, and that's why they're leaving me? But I had to hold me ground to get me house.

One day the postman came with a big letter. John came out to see me—he was working at a garage in the town—and I give him the letter. "Mammy," he said, "it's a letter for you."

"It won't be money," I said. And I was wondering where this big letter was coming from because I wasn't writing to anyone at the time and no one knew me address because I was living on the road. "It must be the family allowance," I said. "It must be about me book. I lost me book."

"Oh," said John, "you got your wish."

"What?" About me book?"

"No," said John, "you got your house."

I didn't believe him first. I got all excited then—I was raging. I didn't know what to do. I was rejoiced!

X I

The Old One

Whenever I drove to Finglas, the crowded housing estate to which Nan moved, I took the long route in order to drive through the Phoenix Park and catch a last glimpse of nature on the way. The estate offered nothing, except a dreary vista of two-story terraces, no trees, and litter everywhere. It was a new area, built on the outskirts of the old village, itself engulfed by the city. The families who lived there were transfers from inner-city flats.

It was the domain of stout women wearing tweed coats, head scarves, and short rubber boots; of worn-thin men in caps and shiny-kneed suits; of boys with shaven heads and heavy leather boots; of young girls with peroxided hair. There was a monotony about the place. Even the children playing in the street amid the dogs and broken glass seemed a uniform height, about three feet.

One seventy-seven Kippure Drive was the second house in on the first street of the estate and close enough to the periphery to have a view of the tip and of the grass and trees beyond. Nan's house was gray, with dark blue trim and a blue door, and indistinguishable from the rest except that Michael and John had built a picket fence around the tiny front garden, and Nan had planted rose bushes. She would have preferred a cottage on her own, like the tiny stone one I passed on my way to visit her, but at Nan's age and in declining health, she was glad of any house.

When Nan walked outside her door, a rare occurence, she could look beyond the estate and see a barrel-top wagon and bender tent belonging to a Travelling family fresh from the country. Down the hill, next to the little stone bridge over the Tolka River sat another Traveller camp. The same family had been living there for years, dealing in scrap metal and second-hand trailers which were jammed together, like pieces in a jigsaw puzzle, on a narrow wedge of land next to the stream bed. Mickey Browne, a nephew of Nan's first husband, was said to do a good business in these and other urban enterprises, including loan sharking—or so other Travellers whispered. Nan told me the view made her lonely and later I was to know why.

Like all Corporation housing, Nan's house was small—just two rooms and a hall on the ground floor and three tiny bedrooms and a bath upstairs. When I visited, we spent most of our time in the parlor—the nicest and warmest room in the house. Nan had papered the walls in a muted pattern of pink and green flowers on a beige background and decorated with a careful symmetry which was evident everywhere, from the twin brass candle sticks and identical figurines of a woman in old-fashioned dress that had been placed at either end of the tiny mantle, to the framed greeting card of a little girl hugging a kitten which hung perfectly centered above it. A large color photograph of Sally, Brendan, and Sally's three children hung on an adjacent wall, above a home-made stand holding an alignment of ceramic horses and vases filled with plastic flowers. The people in the photograph looked happy and neat.

But pictures are often deceiving, and Sally, then twenty-six years old, had bad kidneys; her brother Brendan was filling in for Billy, who had been crippled in a car accident; and the children were in care.

Two battered suitcases on the floor contained all Nan's important papers as well as family snapshots and letters. She had the "look" of each document memorized and could pick out each child's birth certificate and distinguish the old ESB bills from the court summons and TV rental agreement. She worried when she didn't immediately find her free butter book, her deserted wife's allowance book—which entitled her to £22 a week—or the children's allowance book which gave her £4 a month each for Brendan and Eddie until they turned sixteen.

Next to the suitcases sat the television set, the most important object in the house. I often arrived to find Nan and the boys watching Tarzan or a cowboy or gangster film. Next to the telly stood a tall glass-doored case filled with untouched sets of drinking glasses. Centered on the wall above it was a portrait of Our Lord and grouped around him, three soul-eyed Mexican children, a trio of rearing horses on velvet, a flamenco dancer, and a postcard of O'Connell Street.

Its size should have made the house cozy, but it was not. The central heating unit was too costly to run, and in winter a rush of cold air escaped from somewhere behind it. John and Michael complained to the Corporation once but nothing was done, so they searched and found a hole in the floor and plugged it with rags and for the next few years the blast was reduced to a steady draft. A small vinyl-covered couch and easy chair provided the only places to sit. Sheer nylon curtains blocked out a surprising amount of light from the large picture window but they are an Irish decorating convention and also kept out the curious looks of passers-by. As soon as the sun went down, even in summer, Brendan insisted that the heavier drapes be drawn too. Sally once bought a piece of second-hand blue carpeting to cover the linoleum floor and make the room "homely," but she refused to put it down because Kathleen and her husband John tramped in mud from the fields they were camped in.

It was here that Nan spent her days, smoking harsh filterless Woodbines through orange-stained fingers, while sipping sugar-laced tea. At fifty-six she was wrinkled beyond her years, although her long brown hair was only slightly gray.

Her children called her "the old one." And with missing teeth
and a bad chest, she seemed not long for this world. The way
Nan sat said as much; she always perched on the edge of the
couch as if she didn't intend to stay. Only when she was sick,
did her body seemed resigned to its resting place. Then she
lay deep in the couch and coughed—agonizingly long, con-
gested coughs followed by a gulp. On such days it was easy
to feel the boredom and loneliness that Nan and other housed
Travellers complained of, the claustrophobia of looking "at
the four walls" day after day.

YOU'RE NEVER free in a house, you're in prison. You're
always trying to keep everyone happy. When you go out
your door, you don't know whether your neighbour will be
civil or not. If you have a cat and it only jumps over the wall,
you could be attacked over it. And if you have a little dog,
well, there's murder outside: "He's gone in on top of me
flowers!" And there you are, out apologizing. And even your
child, if he only looks crooked at the neighbors, they'll complain. And if he's not properly dressed of a Sunday, one of
them will gab to the others behind your back and if they see
you coming, they'll stare at you and hold their nose up.

Like other Travellers housed in the midst of settled people, Nan kept to herself and had very little to do with her
neighbors. They were friendly enough, but she knew no one
wanted a "tinker" or "knacker" living next door. "They don't
like the Travelling People up here, Sharon," she said more
than once.

THEY CAN'T bear them. I hear them speaking when I'm on
the bus: "Look at them knackers down there. They should

be put out." I pretend I'm real deaf but I do be listening and I can feel it in me face. I'm very pale, but I know me face reddens up when I hear them talk about Travellers.

I was coming home with Michael and John not long after moving into the house. We'd gone to town with a few bob to do a bit of shopping and we were coming home happy, talking about the house—about what color wallpaper we were going to get next week and about paint for the kitchen. "I'll get flowers for the garden," I was saying, and we were in great heart thinking about getting home and having a nice feed.

I had on me good coat, and John and Michael was tidy and clean, but down below us was this man and woman— Travellers—and they were down getting copper and brass out of the dump. Michael knew them but he didn't look over at them because these settled men were standing right beside us. The men were taking down timber from the back of a lorry and we had to stop and wait for them to get it down because there was traffic going by in the street and we couldn't walk by. So we stood there talking about the house.

Then didn't this fella say to John, "Look at them dirty knackers!" pointing to the man and woman in the dump. I looked down at them, but I never opened me mouth. And John didn't say anything. But I could see him getting as red as a turkey top. "Here last week," your man says to him, "Jim here took off his working boots—isn't that right, Jim?— he only had them two weeks and he just left them down and put on his light shoes to run up to the shops for cigarettes. He just left down his working boots after paying a good price for them, and one of them bleeding bastards took them. If I had my way, I'd burn them knackers out. They have more than the people in the houses. See the trailers they have," he said to John and Michael, "and big fancy cars and still they rob. And look what we're earning a week and look how we're sweating for it. If I could know the fella that took these boots, I'd get him. Bleeding tinkers!"

"I wouldn't blame them," said Michael. "Aren't they right," he said, "when they can get things for nothing? Don't you know the price of things today. They'd be bigger fools if they didn't take them. Weren't they right, when he was a fool to leave his boots down?"

"My God," the man looked at Michael then, "don't get that into your head. It'll never happen again, I'll get it out of one of them knackers yet." Finally the last piece of timber came down.

"Come on, John," I said.

"But Michael kept telling the men, "Aren't they right? . . . They're not fools. . . . You'd do the same." When we got to the house I had no heart to look at the paint.

"If the neighbours ever find out we're knackers," I said, "we're done." When we moved into the house first, the neighbors didn't know we was Travellers because we had ourselves dressed up like all the Travellers does. We were all tidy and any little things that we had—blankets, a mattress, not much—we moved in the night. But me neighbours were real nosy. They were loving to get to speak to me. But first I'd just only bid them the time of day and then I'd try to shun them. I didn't like to get too much involved with them. But after, when I'd be putting up me washing on the line in the back, and the neighbour would be spreading out her line and she'd start to speak to me . . . well, I couldn't walk away then. So I'd speak back and be friendly. Finally they asked me what part did I come from. Did I come from the flats in town?

"No, I don't come from the flats," I said, "I was a Traveller. I was only on the road in an old wagon." It was better to let them know straight because they'd find out other ways. I used to hear me children out playing, yelling, "*Corb* the *sublya,* Brendan. *Corb* him!" [Beat the boy, Brendan, Beat him.] and all like this. Well, the neighbors would nearly know you're a Traveller then. And if I'd told people lies and said that I came from the other side of the city or the flats, through time they'd find out and they'd say, "What sort of an upstart is that one, that she's ashamed of who she is? And she's a liar along with it." So I explained to them, and they said, "It must be hard on the road."

I told them it was lovely in the summer but hard in the winter if you haven't a good caravan. And that it's a bit small if you have a big family. And that the caravans is very dear, so you couldn't afford to buy two of them. And a tent is rough on the kids. And they asked me how I liked the house, and I told them, "Oh, I'm proud of it." And so I was.

The only thing about the house I don't like, Sharon, is the worry of money. When I moved in, there wasn't a bit of wallpaper on the walls. The only color that was inside the house was white—roofs and all—and outside, the door was done in blue. And I had no furniture. But I had one great friend, the St. Vincent de Paul. Michael got on to them, and they gave me three beds and two blankets and sheets for each bed. And then they gave me a table and a few chairs and a three-piece suite. And then they got me a gas cooker, that was the most thing I needed. I was real happy then and I started getting the curtains, the paint, the wallpaper meself.

But the cost of living is very hard. The rent when I first came was three pound a week. And the twenty-two pound from the deserted wives' allowance just keeps me bare going from one week to the other. And in the winter it's very hard to manage. A bag of coal is three pound, and we need near two bags a week. The central heating is here but the bill's too high, so we don't have a drop of hot water. I paid sixteen pound for the last gas bill—it comes every two months—and I'm only using the cooker, that's all. Me electric bill is very high. The last one was twenty-two pound and it was just the telly, the washing machine, and the lights. But now me washing machine is broke, so it mightn't be so high the next time. And I pay five pound a month on the television. They sent a bill and I wasn't able to pay it—I'm going to try to pay that next week. That's the way, Sharon. I'm just barely able to live. The twenty-two pound is barely enough for food. I'll have to start the old times again, get candles, wall lamps, a can of parafin oil, a few turfs and start cookin' on an open fire, the way I was reared.

If I had rough and ready neighbors, I wouldn't be so fussy and I'd be more happier, I'd settle better in the house. That's the only thing I don't like about where I am— although they're nice people—they want everything so grand. It gets on my nerves. I'd rather take somebody like meself—poor and rough and ready. But no, the people here want grandeur: different sorts of curtains, different sorts of carpets, lovely three-piece suites. A nice wooden chair wouldn't do them. They like to be posh. They want to be better than their neighbor. But they don't own those things; it's all from the club man. He keeps a book and gives them a card, and they pay two pound a week. That's how a lot of them in the houses gets their things. Anything for a flash.

Even some of me daughters-in-law can be very stuck up. An old woman, a Travelling woman, knocked at the door once. John's wife was there, Teresa, and she answered it. I could hear this woman saying, "Could I have a bit of sugar, I'm making a cup of tea down the road." What I used to say meself when I was short. But Teresa shut the door.

"Who's that at the door?" I said.

"Some old Travelling woman, and the old thing put her foot in the door," Teresa said.

"Listen here," says I. I got very annoyed with Teresa then. "That could be my cousin you're after putting out. The biggest half of them Travelling People is belonging to me, belonging to me mother's side." Well, Teresa didn't know which way to look. So I brought the woman in, and we had a long chat. "Come here," I said to Teresa.

"This is me daughter-in-law," says I to the woman, "she's from Donegal."

"I never seen a good person come from Donegal yet,"

the old woman said. She was vexed. "It's the hungriest county in the world, the county Donegal. Hungry Donegal!" Well, Teresa's face went red.

"I traveled Donegal too and I didn't find them all that bad," I said. "They were very good to me."

"I don't know," says she, "you must be blessed with holy water or something if they were good to you. They eat skins and all down there, hungry Donegal." We were having a laugh at Teresa, we only done it for fun.

"I'm never going near that door again if any Travelling Person comes," Teresa said after.

"You're lucky she didn't catch you be the head and beat you again the ground," I said. Ever after, Teresa'd look and if she seen anybody coming she'd say, "Nan, there's somebody coming," and she'd let me answer the door.

City people can be very thick and ignorant. I got very annoyed once, Sharon. I went into the flats with Eddie to see Sally and we went in to a pub. Billy, me son-in-law, took us. We had ourselves a drink and after, Sally left me at the bus with Eddie. And when I got on, didn't I walk up to the top and there was three skin-head fellas sitting there. They had their little bottle of cider and the three of them were sharing it. I sat down, lit me cigarette and I was smoking and taking no notice of them but I could hear them tittering. There was some girls with them, and they were all grinning and laughing, "Look at the knackers."

"God!" I said to Eddie, letting them know I was getting annoyed about it. "They're very happy now. They must have gettin' three bottles of cider instead of the one. Is today dole day? Cause it's only on dole day that they're able to get their cheap sup of cider, and they must think now that they're millionaries—the little pups."

"You're only a knacker," one of them said.

"Yes," I said, "thanks for calling me that. You're after making me very proud because a knacker has respect. If it was a few knacker young fellas up here in this bus tonight, they wouldn't make fun of an old person. They were better reared than that. Yous are the scruff of Dublin, it's yous that is half starved from one week to the other. Every shilling you get, you have to hand it down to the club man for your little suits. And just because you're a skinner, you think everyone is afraid of you."

Well, there was a respectable aged man on the far side of the bus with his son and he said, "Leave that woman alone."

I got off the bus then and went home and told the boys about it. "You're worse than them," Michael said, "an old woman giving sense to children." But these skinners were no children, Sharon, they were from seventeen up to twenty-two years of age. They were grown up men.

Incidents like this were not new and as it turned out, they were the least of Nan's troubles. The next summer I returned to find that Nan had moved. I walked down treelined Oaklands Drive, past suburban homes and through a large set of black metal gates. The gray stucco and stone house and manicured lawns were pleasant enough; like so many in Ireland, the hospital had once been an estate. Nevertheless, I entered the front hall with trepidation not knowing how ill Nan would be. The ward was silent, the patients lying in their beds like shipwrecked survivors in a sea of white.

"I didn't know what was wrong," Nan whispered as I leaned over her bed, the rest of the patients straining with undisguised curiosity to hear us.

But I began to get very weak and I couldn't eat and I was dizzy in me head. I was a long time sick but I didn't go to the doctor first because I was waiting on me medical card. Then Sally told her own doctor on Harcourt Street about me, and he said to bring me in. So I went in and when he saw me, he said, "You're very bad. It couldn't be much worse. The only thing you can do now is go straight to the Rotunda in the morning—something serious is wrong, so promise me you'll go."

Well, that scared me and I went. He gave me a letter, and I went to the hospital and handed it to a doctor and got a bed straight away. And the next morning a nice lady doctor came and she told me that I had cancer, womb cancer, and that I'd have to come under an operation. But they said the cancer was just starting—it was just like the top of a cigarette—and if I went through the operation, I'd be saved before it spread. So I went for the operation, there was no other choice.

I was three weeks in the Rotunda, then they sent me here to St. Luke's. When I heard I was coming to St. Luke's, I got worried because this is all a cancer hospital, and I thought, I must be very bad. But when I got here, the doctor shook me hand and said, "We'll take good care of you. We're getting you in time."

Nan stayed at St. Luke's for several weeks that summer, undergoing another operation and radiation treatment. I visited her often. Sometimes we talked in the visitor's room but it was always smoky and had the television blaring, so if the weather was fine, we went outside and sat on one of the ornate cast-iron benches facing the tennis courts.

After a while Nan was well enough to go home on weekends. Her first Saturday back, she was visited by her nephew John—one of Pat's sons. "I know a great place where you can get cured," he told her, "but you have to have the belief. If you have no belief, you'd be better to stay at home. It'd be unlucky for you to come." And then he told her all about St. Bridget's Well outside Mullingar.

"Sure, I know all about it," Nan said. "Several people is after being cured in it, but anyone that went to it and didn't

believe, didn't live long after. That really is the truth, Sharon.
I knew a few that didn't live long after."

The next Saturday John was at Nan's door at seven in the
morning. With Kevin, they piled into his battered Ford escort
van and headed for Mullingar, detouring to Rochfortbridge,
a tiny village a few miles south, to visit a "curing priest." Three
curing priests were well-known among Travellers. It's difficult to say how the relationships began, but the priests were
believed to have almost magical powers to cure Travellers
and were visited frequently.

You're supposed to ring this old priest to make an
appointment because he's away a lot and he's very busy,
"but we didn't and for the luck of God, when we went to
the door he answered it. The priest just opened the door—
me nephew John couldn't believe it—and he brought us in
to this big room and we had a talk. "You've come here to
see me," he said to me, "are you sick?"
    "I am Father."
    "You've come a long way?"
    "From Dublin." And I started telling him about St. Luke's
Hospital and about me cancer. And I told him, "Father, I
have another operation to go through."
    Well, this old priest started saying all these prayers in
Latin and then he said so many Hail Marys, Our Fathers, and
the Act of Contrition, and we answered him back. Me and
Kevin and John was on our knees in his room. Then he told
Kevin to take out his rosary beads when he got home and to
say the rosary every night while I was in hospital and not to
miss one night. I got a bit scared when I heard this, thinking
what if the boys goes to the pictures and Kevin gets tired
and falls asleep and forgets the rosary. But the old priest
told me, "You go back to the hospital and you'll be cured.

You'll live for a good many years, you needn't worry. God speed."

Now I was very weak and I wasn't expecting to live, Sharon. You know the way doctors just try to cheer you up when you're really sick. But after seeing this old priest I begin to feel a bit better. We went on to St. Bridget's Well then.

You'd know there was something good at that well by the look of it. There's this little chapel with about eight stones around it, like headstones with writing on them. It must be thousands of years back when those stones was put at this well. And there's a cup and when I took the cup and drank the water, it was like ice. I went down and prayed all around the headstones then, and we filled up about seven or eight lemonade bottles then with this water to bring back. I took one out to the hospital; I had it in me locker beside me bed.

When I returned in 1978, Nan's health was much the same. She had good days and bad. On some visits the mood in the house was cheerful, but much of the time it was sad. Traveller life, in the city at least, always struck me as slightly sad. Whether living in a camp or in a house, people spent most of their time sitting or carrying out routine tasks at a slow rate—tinkering with an engine, washing clothes, poking the fire, borrowing a broom—while waiting for dramatic news. And when the news came, it was usually bad and only sometimes funny or good. Then action would be taken—a quick trip to the country, a race across town, a dash to the pub. One time I arrived to visit Nan only to find that she had flown to England with her son-in-law John in response to a letter from her daughter Mary.

Sometimes I arrived to find the house a shambles, with scattered tea mugs and Guinness bottles, cigarette butts and bread ground into the floor, and Nan, with matted hair and wrinkled clothes, perched on the edge of her chair. No matter how she had been feeling, if friends of the boys arrived or her son James brought over drink, the party went on for hours and even if she had been able to leave the room without making them angry, she would not have been able to sleep. As she said herself, she was no longer "able for it."

"I'm anything but strong," Nan confided to me on one such morning. Brendan and Eddie were upstairs in bed. It was bleak outside and the house felt damp and cold.

I'm NEARLY all the time sick now. My chest is getting bad and I get more pains than ever. I used to be able to run— you'd often see me running through the ditches when Mick would come home drunk—but now I can't walk to the top of that road. I just walk a little way and all of the sudden here I am holding me chest trying to catch me breath. It's too many cigarettes. I think it's the house too—I'm too stuffed up.

Oh, it's an awful thing to be sick, Sharon. I can't bear noise or anything around me then. I get very contrary and I give out to the kids. And I get fed up looking at things piling up and not being able to work, but I hate to ask anybody to sweep up the place or make a bed. Only for Brendan and Eddie, I'd be very let down. They do their best, but me daughters-in-law and daughters aren't very helpful. They just come in and then away again. None of them realize. They think that if I'm able to get on me feet at all, that I'm still young and well.

This winter is after getting me down terrible, Sharon. My God, once I lived through this winter, I think I'll live a long time! I never thought it could happen to me. Here I was with Brendan and Eddie in the house. Then Brendan went

down to Ballymun to stay with Kevin and Tish, and James
came and brought Eddie away for Christmas, to give him a
good time out. So here I was, left on me own.

Just then the little picture of a child and kitten crashed to
the floor, landing on the tile hearth. We both jumped. "I'll
have to destroy that picture, Sharon," Nan said in an irritated
voice. "It's after falling three times now and it's bringing me
no luck. Little Nanzer give me that, but grandchild or no, I'm
going to destroy it." She reached over and tossed it into the
fire, frame and all.

WELL, IT was a very bad winter and what happened? First
the pipes busted, then the coalmen went on strike. I had no
fire and no water. I was three days in the house without a
cup of tea—I hadn't even a sup of water. And for me own
bad luck didn't I take real bad with me chest. The pains
were terrible. There was a drop of milk and I took the drop
of cold milk and then I got a blanket and I just lay on that
old sofa and tried to keep meself. I was near freezin. I
thought to get a taxi but I wasn't able to get to the door. And
I didn't like the idea of bothering me neighbours. You know
the way people talk, and I knew they'd say, "Well, she had a
crowded house and now when she needs them, she has
nobody." So I said to meself, I'll try to get over it, and I
waited and I started praying. I prayed mostly for God to
send somebody.

And for the luck of God, didn't Kevin come down and the
very minute he did, he got a taxi and took me down to Ballymun. I collapsed with the flu. I stayed there with Kevin
and Tish a couple weeks. I'll never forget it. To think a thing
like that can happen when you've reared a big family and
have grandchildren and all. I always thought I'd have some-

body around, but when you get old or sick, I don't think anybody wants you.

Fortunately, Nan was seldom truely alone. The small house had an ever changing occupancy of sons, daughters, daughters-in-law, and visitors; and her two youngest sons, Brendan and Eddie, were almost always there.

FAMILIES IS terrible comical. I think the young people today don't really have the same nature for their fathers and mothers, no respect for them, as we did. They don't listen to their parents. A child only comes to twelve year old, and they try to walk all over their parents. And when they come to fifteen or sixteen years, they want to get away. You wouldn't blame them, if they could do something good for themselves. Then you'd love to see them going and you'd shove them out the door. But you don't like to see your children leaving you and going into worse. That's the worry a mother has.

I'm all the time telling the kids—the boys—to keep off the road. "There's nothing on the road," I say. Because a person would want to be strong and very good-brained to live on the road. Travelling men and women are very clever people, you know, although they don't know how to read or write their name. Let them at anything and they'll make a living. Leave down ten pound, and the smallest Travelling child can count out every penny of it. So I told my kids, "You're not quick enough or good enough to be a Traveller." I keep telling them to get a job and settle down, but they've turned on me now and tell me to mind me own business. I get meself insulted over advising them. So now, I'll just let them find out for themselves.

What made me want to get off the road was the kids. I

didn't want them to get it as hard as I got it. They weren't real strong and I used to worry that the winter would kill them. I always wanted to get a roof over their heads. I was always fighting hard for a home to get them a bit of education, and so's if they ever got a job, they'd have an address. I had a lovely house in England, I done me best in Galway, and now, thank God, I have a house.

I was proud of John when he married his little girl, Teresa. She wasn't a Traveller. John never wanted the road because he knew he wasn't strong enough. John's brained enough but he wasn't really fit for the road life. So I was happy when he settled down and he's still settled. I got a letter from Willie, he's living in London now and married to a settled girl. I have no worry about them two, any time I want them, I know where to find them because I have an address. That's the nice thing about a house, even if it's rented, it's still a home over your head and you'll always be able to find out where one another is. I've lost a lot of me parent's people that was on the road—I can't really say where me uncles went or lots of me aunts.

Me son Joe's settled too. He travelled when he was young but he was a great scholar, passed primary and all, and he was in the army. I haven't heard from Joe this long time but when I took sick with cancer, the hospital began searching for him. A few months ago I heard he was the manager over a hotel in London and that he's married to an Irish lady a bit older than himself and has two children.

Me daughter Mary is living in a flat in Birmingham. She's doing fine—married to a nice Irish fella. I like her husband, he was all over me, friendly and nice, the last time I was there. But something very peculiar is going on. I don't understand it. When I went to Birmingham this last time to see Mary, she had her arm broke. It was all black and blue with this bone sticking out. I said, "Mary what happened to your arm?"

"Oh, I got that broke in the convent, mother."

"Mary," I said, "I'm sorry for contradicting you but that's only after happening. It's all blue. I seen you when you were working in Dublin, with your sleeves rolled up, and there was no bone like that." But she didn't answer me. She was scared of her husband. I'm worrying about Mary now.

Eileen's married in Anderstown in the North to a settled fella. Sally married Billy, another settled fella, and she won't travel. She and Billy lived on the road, but Sally'd rather have the flats. Kevin married a settled girl, Tish, and he wouldn't have the road life. Kevin's not strong anyway, although he's smart, and he's a bit lazy. Kathleen married John, one of me sister Maggie's sons, but he was reared in a house in Birmingham. They're in a trailer now because John thinks the road is exciting. But this is his first experience on the road, and I wouldn't say he'd stay long. He's used to his clean clothes and his baths. He comes back here to me and says, "I feel scruffy. Will you switch on the water till I get a bath? I haven't a bath for a long time." He'll feel more of that again before he's finished with the road. I wouldn't say he'd put up with the road long.

Some of me kids is on the road—James and Michael. James was well educated, in the army and all, but he likes the Travelling life. He and Mary are all the time on the road and now they have ten kids. I used to pray to God that when Michael'd get married, he'd marry a settled girl and get a little home so he wouldn't be slaved on the road. "Even if she's made some mistakes, forgive her," I told him. "She'll turn out all right in the end." I thought Michael was going to do better for himself than he did. I'd have liking to see him get a steady job and a home, so he'd have a place to bring his children up right. But he didn't. He married a Travelling girl, one of Mick's brother's daughters, and moved on to the road.

I really couldn't say what me last kids will do. Sam is more like a settled person than a Traveller, although he does a lot of travelling with his karate. He has medals and ribbons and all. Sam's very clever, although be times you wouldn't think it, and he can read and write. He hates the travelling life. He was living in a flat in the city and working for Chinese people in a restaurant. But now he's doing karate."

Brendan give up his bar job, Sharon. Did I tell you that? Now, isn't that a pity. I told him, "Don't worry about your wages, Brendan, you're getting your training. And you'll get a reference and then you're right for the rest of your life because a barman can go anywhere and get a job. And you're in and you're dry all the time, and you have nothing to do, only keep yourself clean and well-dressed." A bar job was better than working like poor Michael out in the buildings, slaved with heavy work and frost and you're only wanted for six months and then he has to go on looking for another job. But Brendan give it up. It was too early a job and too steady. He liked it but he couldn't stick it. I don't know which life Brendan will end up with.

Just then Brendan and a friend came in. They had just bought a wrecked car and were going to strip it for parts. I asked Brendan why he had quit his job at the airport, and he said the people were "too posh" and he didn't like talking to them. I could imagine his discomfort as he stood before me, gawky and thin, wearing a thick leather belt covered in shiny metal studs at the waist of his grease-stained pants. "You should only go up, Brendan," Nan said. "Never try to go down. You should always try to better yourself." But Brendan wasn't listening and soon he and his friend walked out.

"Do you want more tea, Sharon?" Nan asked.

"No, I'm fine." I'd already had three cups. But Nan shouted for Eddie anyway, and a minute later he walked in, grinning sheepishly.

"Eddie, put on the kettle and run to the shops and get us some biscuits, some cream ones. And buy me ten Woodbines."

"Do you want Jacobs?" he asked, trying to get it right.

"Just get some nice ones," Nan said. Eddie took the crumpled pound note and left the room, but not before Nan tucked his shirttail in and ordered him to wash his face and hands. A second later, we heard the front door open, a blur of childrens' voices, and then a slam.

EDDIE, NOW, is very childish, a little fella of six—as true as God, Sharon—has more sense. He'll be sixteen in July, the third of July, but he goes on with the smallest children here. And such foolish ways. I keep telling him, "Eddie, you're going to have to grow up. You're very childish." And I try to teach him what to do. One minute you see him doing something sensible, then he's back into the childish ways again. I took the brush to him a couple of times, just to try and get sense into him. I got tired of petting him—"Now Eddie, do this. . . . Now Eddie, don't touch that." So I took up the brush where I was sweeping and hit him on the top of the back, "Get out! You're going too far!" Eddie might turn yet, he might change. I don't know. It's just your luck, that's all. But I do worry about Eddie. I'd love to live as long as I could to see Eddie a few year more.

I'll die a Traveller and be proud to be a Traveller but I wouldn't like me children to travel. It's a feeling I have, Sharon, because the road is different now. You can't go around the country selling today the way we used to. The farmers won't buy anything off a Traveller, and they don't need a tinsmith or a sweep. Years ago we could walk into any wood and put up our camp, but if a farmer only sees you getting a few sticks to make a fire today, he's down on top of you with a gun. That's why Travellers is packed into cities today. There's nothing in the country.

And the Travelling People is changed too. They used to be harmless and innocent, they believed in nothing only telling stories. But they've gone spiteful and jealous. They don't like to see anyone getting more than they've got and they like to harm people through telling lies and trying to rise trouble. That's one thing I hate, I hate anyone to tell me a lie. I'd rather a robber than a liar, because a robber won't do you much harm but a liar could get you kilt.

No, travelling wouldn't be the same at all today. I wouldn't like it for my family—it'd be too rough for them. So I'd rather they settled down and get a good job, even a middling job, and keep a constant home.

Isn't it comical how things change. I loved the travelling life, although I got it very hard. You mightn't believe this, Sharon, but if I was young and somebody said, "Here's a little farm and here's money. That's your home now for life. You can have all that or else go on the way you are." Well, I'd rather be a Traveller. Because I can say what a lot of farmers can't, that I've travelled all Ireland and I've travelled parts of England. They had money but they hadn't the guts to leave Ireland or even their own county. But I've travelled every part, and seen different sceneries, talked with different people, done different work. I had freedom and me own enjoyment and me mind wasn't gone stupid from looking at the one place all the time.

I think it an awful thing to stay in a farm, just to walk around the one yard, do the same thing day after day, never to leave that farm, and to die and be buried there. I wouldn't have it. Ask any Traveller that's a few year in a house. The only thing that breaks a Traveller's heart is when March comes and then May and the birds are out early in the morning and the fields get lovely and green and the bushes are green. Well, to hold yourself in a house then, where you get no open air and you're waiting for the gas man and waiting for your electric bills and waiting for this to be done and that and you're only going from one room to another. It's miserable.

But when you're out in the country, you see all the sceneries—lovely woods and lakes, sheep and cows, every sort

of bird. Coming around Easter in the farmyards, it's lovely to
see the farmers' wives feeding the hens and young chickens
and ducks—you hear them cackling. You go from one
county to another and meet different people, every class
and every sort. And even if you don't speak to them, you're
looking at them. We used to meet some terrible bad people
when we were travelling, right enough, but you get over that
and before long, you meet kind people that you'd love for
company, people that when you'd part with them, you'd be
lonely. I'd rather mix with everybody and take me chances.

When I see a trailer or a wagon or a tent, I think freedom.
Freedom and people going up and down saying "Hello,"
"How are you?" "Good morning," "It's a grand day." I'd love
to get me basket again and go round selling to the doors,
just to have a talk with the people and see different things,
their gardens, and what they have. And the old Travelling
People were the best-hearted people, there was kindness
and truth in them. They were real Irish people. They were
poor but they didn't care about money and once they had
enough to eat and their bed and some way of getting along,
they were thankful to God for that.

If I was travelling again, I wouldn't go into towns or near
a city. They're not healthy; there's too much smoke. You
think you're getting fresh air in a city—you're not. And cities
are nothing only trouble for anyone rearing a young family.
Because when you're poor, your children meets in with
poorer again and then they start getting into trouble. But in
the country they won't go wrong on you because they meet
no bad company and they'll always have something to do.
They can go off and enjoy themselves playing in the fields,
picking up sticks, or washing themselves in a stream or fishing. A child always has something to do in the country. I'd
rather be in a tent at the side of a woods than in a town.

If I really knew I'd live another five year, I'd be on the
road again. If I was young and strong, I'd still go that life—
the travelling life—but I'd go a different way. I'd like to be a

bit better off and more happier. I wasn't so happy. And I wouldn't go with the cruelty I went through.

Oh, I had an awful mixup of a life. I was always coming and going. I never was really settled. No matter what I used to have or what I'd do, I never could say, "Well, I'm here now and I'm settled." And all the breaking up with me marriage and with Mick. My God, when I think back on it . . . I'd rather not think back on it. I suffered an awful lot because I never knew when I was going to be left on me own. A man like Mick or Browne could get up, and so they used to, and walk away and I could do nothing about it because of the kids. I had to look after them. Mick was free to come and do as he liked, but not me. It's very hard to try and rear a family on your own, without money. I'd have to go out and try to sell and if I had a bad day, I had all this worry. And if one of the children got sick, I had to get it to a doctor or the hospital.

I had a harder life than any other Travelling woman. They classed it a hard life if they got a bit of a bashing up by their husbands. But they hadn't to do what I had to do to rear me family, and then me kids being taken. I don't really think I had a happy time from the day I got married.

"Isn't the evening times very lonely, Sharon," Nan said, after a long silence. It was late in the afternoon, nearly dusk, and we were both tired. The house was silent and empty. Yellow light cut across the room, jumping across Nan's hands, highlighting their many wrinkles and blackened pores. She twirled her teacup absently, and I sat thinking that had I seldom seen her hands empty. "When I sit here," Nan continued, " just right where I am, I get lonesome. Do you see that old road coming down and the little bridge, right where they're building a new way? It makes me lonesome and sad to look at it."

THERE'S SOME nights when the boys go to bed, I sit here—I often sat here to about two o'clock in the morning—and I look out that window and everything comes back. And even in the day I sit here and I do be thinking. Peter, me nephew, was here the other day and he said, "You're always looking out through that window. Every time I come in, you're looking out it and you don't want to speak to us. You make me miserable." I do be thinking all the time, and I might be speaking to the boys, gabbing, real happy, and then they'll say, "Did you hear about . . ." And I wouldn't hear them at all because me mind is going back, back through me life. Oh, this is the truth Sharon, I look out that window and me whole life comes back.

I never told any of them, but just there at that corner there's a wide spot where me and Mick used to stay. They call that bridge Broom Bridge. I never forgot the name of it—and I'm after going to England and forgetting a lot of things. I never forgot the name of it because I was always nervous going over it. It's a very dangerous bridge. Did you go over it? It's right at the bottom of a sharp corner. Years ago when we were staying there, we'd be coming back out from the city and I used to get scared to death driving the pony over that bridge. When Mick used to have a few drinks taken, he was a very dangerous driver. And I'd be on the cart with the kids and I'd be praying and praying. Me nerves used to be gone with that bridge. Coming back on a dark winter night, it was the loneliest road. You wouldn't see nothing.

I remember Mary, she was eight year old at that time. I remember lots of things now with Mary, the dolls she used to have and the old sayings. She was very old-fashioned, the way she used to speak. There was a little shop just before you got to the bridge. The cottage is still there. There's a garage there now, but that time there was a little shop in the cottage. There wasn't much traffic that time on the road, just a pony and cart with the coalmen coming around or somebody selling timber. And Mary used to walk to that shop and bring our messages back. She was so clever.

Even last night I was sitting here and I could still see Mary. Oh, it makes me terrible lonesome. Isn't it queer the way they put this house, and that this is the house I got. I do think to meself, if I had of getting a different house in Finglas I wouldn't be so lonesome. But to be just here where everything happened.

I never came back to that road after, nor would I, not till I came to this house. I was only just in the house when Kathleen and John, before they were married, were going for a walk and I went with them. I didn't know where I was then because I was years away from this part of Dublin. But when we walked down, up, and around that road and we went to the bridge, I was near crying. I know where I am now, I said to meself but I didn't say nothing to Kathleen and John. And just near the bridge I took a little weed of a tree, an elder— the root of it—and put it in me pocket. And when I come back to the house, I planted it up against the shed. It was that small that you'd never think it'd grow, but didn't it grow so high it topped the shed. And now it gets all these white blossoms and berries.

I got it for a remembrance.

Just there was where everything happened. Just there at that corner was a wide spot where we used to stay. And just there, that's where Mary, Joe, Sally, John, Willie, and Eileen was when me brother Pat came and took them away. My life was never really any good after. And I remember Mick walking away up that road and me watching him go around the bend. And then I went on with Pat to Mullingar, and that was the last of me little family. After the kids was taken, I never could bear that road. For years I wouldn't go near it, and now I'm looking at it every day. Isn't it cruel and comical how life turns out.

I had a very hard life. I was poor and I made mistakes. Still, I done me best and I'm proud of meself. I never regretted. Whatever I done, I put up with it. Because it's all for life, it's all left out for you—that's how I look into it. I think from the day you're born, it's left there—marked down for you—and you just have to go through it. That's the way I believe. Whatever you are, whatever you do, you'd still do the same thing if you were born over again. You just go through whatever the Lord leaves you. And for me, I was a Traveller on the road.

Epilogue

The path was dark. Towering copper beeches linked branches high overhead, their deep maroon leaves rustling in the wind as we walked. I'd spent the afternoon in Dublin visiting some of Nan's boys—all grown men now—and was on my way to see Nan. Sam and John walked with me. I'd never been to Mt. Jerome before. It was an old place; its residents crowded together, the ancient grey stones jammed against one another. Some had buckled and cracked. Nevertheless, Nan was in good company. Cherubs smiled, Virgins gazed beatifically, Arthur Guinness rested nearby.

The last time I had seen Nan was in the summer of 1981. Now it was 1985, and I missed her. We rounded a corner and followed the path through a break in a garden wall. "She always loved the garden," John said as we emerged into open sunshine. I followed the boys to the far wall and there in the last row, her back to the rest, lay Nan. My throat tightened and my eyes began to burn, as they had two years earlier when Sam had telephoned me with the news. It was a cold March evening in 1983, and I'd been away for two months. "I've been trying to get you," he said, and then I knew. "Mammy died on the eighth of February . . ." Sam was fidgeting now, fighting back tears. John stood still and forlorn. "In loving memory of Our Dear Mother," the shiny black stone read. It was a nice headstone, very similar to the others except for the statue of Our Lady on the left and a small oval photograph of Nan in one corner.

We stood for a few minutes saying nothing. Then John knelt to straighten the glass globes of artificial flowers at the base of the grave, wondering aloud where the two white ceramic doves he had left had gone. Nan had wanted a rose bush planted on her grave, but cemetery rules forbade it. The boys also knew she would have wanted Our Lady's cloak painted blue and gold and debated whether they should do it themselves or pay the cemetery. The cemetery people might do a more professional job they reasoned, although John had always been a good painter.

Not everyone had wanted Nan to lie here. Their cousins and aunts and uncles in Mullingar had insisted that Mullingar was the appropriate place. But John as the eldest son present at the time had taken a vote of the immediate family, and they had decided on Mt. Jerome. Mick was buried here too but in a numbered pauper's grave. Sam and John did not know exactly where, since Mick's eldest sons by his first marriage had handled the burial arrangements.

Several weeks before Nan's death there had been fighting in the house between Nan's sister Maggie's sons, who were over from England, cousins from Mullingar, and some of the neighbors in Finglas. There were allegations of stolen goods, and the boys had been caught in the fighting. John's jaw was broken and his front teeth knocked out. At age thirty-five, gentle John already looked battered and weary of life. "We all wanted to be like mammy, Sharon, but we're all ending up like our dad," he said with a sad, ironic smile. Nan had been forced into the center of the fray. The stress, the lost hours of sleep, the noise and worry, had all worsened her chest. For weeks she had lain on the couch downstairs, too weak to climb the stairs to bed. She finally went to stay at Kevin's flat in Ballymun, caught the flu and then pneumonia, which became so severe that she could hardly breathe. Kevin rang for an ambulance.

Nan lived in the Mater hospital for three weeks. The boys and Sally and Kathleen came to see her every day. To cheer her up, Sam told her he had located her long lost son, Joe— "I think she half believed me." Her eldest son, James, came too but arrived drunk and started a loud argument the night before she died. The boys threatened to kill him if they ever saw him again and after that he dropped out of sight. The doctor told them she should have died years ago. Nan was sixty-three.

"Look, there's a bee. That's a good sign," said John. A bee had landed on a flower at the base of Nan's headstone.

"She's knows we're here and she's happy," said Sam.

"She's contented," added John.

We started to talk about Nan.

"Mammy always used to tell us stories," said Sam. "A bird landed on me shoulder once and mammy said, 'That's good luck. You're going to get money.' And I did. Some money came in a letter the next day. She was a great old lady, a character. . . . She loved her drink but she could get along with everybody. She was loveable and kindhearted. Everybody liked her, didn't they, Sharon?"

"Mammy never hit us because things upset her," said John. "She only hit us if we were going wrong—mixing up with the wrong type of girl or heading for trouble with the law— then she'd hit us with a brush. And the morning after any of us had been out drinking, she'd get up early—mammy always got up very early—and she'd come into the room and tell us what she thought. 'You think you're a big man now, do you?' she'd say. 'Well, I'll fight you. Come on.' And she'd have a fair box at us, just to put a bit of manners into us."

"She was a father as well as a mother," agreed Sam.

I asked them about Mick.

"He wasn't a happy man," John said. "He was a good story-teller and he started to be interested in learning later in life— he'd come over to me when we were living on the site and ask me about different things—but he wasn't a happy man. He was a good man but he had a rough life and he took it out on her. I pitied him, Sharon, for what he was trying to be—his own man. He was trying to find some escape. He was a good tradesman. Daddy was very good with his hands, but he didn't have the education to prove it. He had to go about getting jobs the hard way, and then other people would be above him. He could have amounted to something—we all could—he had a good brain." John stopped, took out a plastic pouch of tobacco and rolled a cigarette. "He was a sentimental man too, only he didn't know how to show love. He couldn't. He was a lonely man."

"I hated him and I loved him," Sam said abruptly. "Once he was very nice to me. He let me sleep in the tent with him after I gave him £10. I'd been out begging—I'd told all kinds of lies about how me father would beat me if I didn't get money—and when I got back, I gave the old fella £10. And he said, 'Good lad.' Then he went off to get booze. But when he came back he gave me two Guinnesses. I felt like a real man sitting there, drinking at the fire with me daddy. It was worth £10,000 to me." Sam paused for a second, "This was just before he died. That was the best time I ever had with him. I never really knew him. I wish I had."

We then talked about why Nan had stayed with Mick through all the beatings and hardship. And why Mick had become so cruel. These were difficult questions, and the three of us stood for over an hour in the warm August sunshine in front of Nan's grave pondering them.

"He was very jealous," John said.

"They were too close in blood," suggested Sam.

"She pitied him," said John.

"She loved him," said Sam.

"She needed him," concluded John.

"How?" I asked.

"She needed him for us kids. Mammy needed the old fella to stand by her. Our relations always condemned us as bastards; mammy's family always threw up 'bastards!' in her face. But mammy would turn around and say to them, 'I'm proud of my bastards.' Too bad we didn't amount to anything, Sharon. Mammy tried to keep us up—to advise us—to prove we could be better than anyone thought. She had pride. She made a mistake with Mick, but she stood by Mick. 'He's not me husband, but he's me man and me kid's father,' she'd say. It made us feel more secure, because he was our dad. When others called us bastards, we knew our dad. Not like some."

Yes, that explained a lot. Staying with Mick had made the whole thing more honorable. No one could accuse Nan of being a loose woman or speculate about her children's parentage as long as Mick was there. Nan had always told me she stayed with Mick "for the sake of the children," but I'd never fully understood. Now, I think I did. Not every gray hair on Nan's head may have been honorably earned, but Nan was an honorable woman.

NOTES

1. This treatment of the Travellers' early history is of necessity short and much more research needs to be done. For a more detailed discussion see Sharon Bohn Gmelch and George Gmelch, "The Emergence of an Ethnic Group: The Irish Tinkers." *Anthropological Quarterly* 49(1976):225–38.
2. According to a 1981 census conducted under the supervision of Dublin's Economic and Social Research Institute, there were 2,432 Travelling families in Ireland. In 1984, according to the 1985 report of the National Council for Travelling People, there were 2,994 families. Given the difficulties in locating and enumerating all Travellers and the periodic migration of some families to England, these figures should be regarded as close approximations. In 1981, there were 110 families living in Northern Ireland and an estimated 800 families in England and Wales.
3. Begging was a major occupation of Travelling women in the 1960s and 1970s. Some women begged for money from passers-by on city sidewalks; others walked from door to door in the suburbs, asking for food and clothing. The latter sometimes developed patroness–client relationships with the housewives they met. In the best of these relationships, social barriers are partially broken down. In conversation, the Travelling woman may relate her family problems. The patroness, in turn, may give friendly advice, write letters and fill-in forms for the Traveller, and help her deal with police, courts, and welfare officials.

   Begging has declined in recent years due apparently to increases in welfare payments and a change in attitude among younger Traveller women, many of whom now regard it as demeaning. For a detailed discussion of the begging strategies used by Travellers during the 1970s see George Gmelch and Sharon Bohn Gmelch, "Begging in Dublin:

The Strategies of a Marginal Urban Occupation." *Urban Life* 6(1978): 66–75.

4. See M. H. Crawford and George Gmelch, "The Human Biology of Irish Tinkers: Demography, Ethnohistory, and Genetics." *Social Biology* 21(1974): 321–31, and M. H. Crawford, "Genetic Affinities and Origin of Irish Tinkers." In *Biosocial Interrelations in Population Adaptation,* edited by E. S. Watts, F. E. Johnston, and G. W. Lasker, pp. 93–103. The Hague: Mouton, 1976.

5. Irish Travellers speak a secret argot or cant known as Gammon. It is used primarily to conceal meaning from outsiders, especially during business transactions and in the presence of police. Most Gammon utterances are terse and spoken so quickly that a non-Traveller might conclude the words merely had been garbled.

Most Gammon words were formed from Irish Gaelic by applying four techniques: reversal, metathesis, affixing, and substitution. In the first, an Irish word was reversed to form a Gammon one—*mac,* or son, in Irish became *kam* in Gammon. In the second, consonants or consonant clusters were transposed. Thirdly, a sound or cluster of sounds were either prefixed or suffixed to an Irish word. Some of the more frequently prefixed sounds were s, gr, and g. For example, *O Bair,* work or job, became *gruber* in Gammon. Lastly, many Gammon words were formed by substituting an arbitrary consonant or consonant cluster for one in the Irish word. In more recent years, modern slang and Romani (the language of the Gypsies) words have been incorporated. The grammar and syntax are English.

The first vocabulary collected from Irish Travellers was published in 1808, indicating that Gammon dates at least to the 1700s. But many early Celtic scholars who studied it, including the eminent Kuno Meyer, concluded it was much older. Meyer's articles can be found in the *Journal of the Gypsy Lore Society* 2 (1891):257–66 and 2(1909):241–46. For a more modern study of Gammon, as spoken by Irish Travellers in the United States, see Jared Harper and Charles Hudson "Irish Traveller Cant." *Journal of English Linguistics* 15(1971):78–86, and "Irish Traveller Cant in its Social Setting." *Southern Folklore Quarterly* 37(1973): 101–14.

6. In 1960 the Irish government established the Commission on Itinerancy to investigate the problems caused by the growing numbers of Travellers then living in urban areas and to recommend solutions. The commission's report, published in 1963, documented for the first time the extent of the poverty and deprivation under which most Travelling families lived. The report and the growing publicity surrounding Dublin Travellers' attempts to resist evictions prompted three influential

settled people—Victor Bewley, Lady Wicklow, and Fr. Thomas Fehily—to organize the first itinerant settlement committee in Dublin in 1965. And so began the national movement to settle Travellers (primarily on official campsites in small, prefabricated bungalows but also in conventional housing). Settlement or housing was seen as the key to the solution of the "itinerant problem." The movement's work also came to include primary education, social work, vocational training, and daycare provision. At the peak of the movement there were over seventy local, volunteer committees. The movement is still active today, although its emphasis on housing and settlement has been toned down.

7. My initial research with Travellers focused on this issue, examining the ways in which Traveller culture differs from that of settled Irish and the type of interaction that takes place between members of the two groups. *(The Emergence and Persistence of an Ethnic Group: The Irish Travellers,* Ph.D. Dissertation, University of California, Santa Barbara, 1974.)

8. For more information on the reasons for the Travellers' urban exodus and the cultural changes that took place as a result of it, see George Gmelch, *The Irish Tinkers: The Urbanization of an Itinerant People.* Prospect Heights, Ill.: Waveland Press, 1985.

9. I began recording Nan's life story in the summer of 1975, although I knew much of its outline from my research with Travellers in 1971–72. In 1976 I returned for a month and following that, for periods of several weeks to three months every year through 1981. I tape recorded twenty-four hours of interviews with Nan; the rest of our many conversations were written up as fieldnotes. It is from the taped interviews that Nan's direct quotations have been edited. The epilogue is based on fieldwork conducted in 1985.

10. November 1 was originally a Celtic feast day—"the night of the evil spirits"—and the traditional start of winter. It later became the Christian feast day of All Soul's.

11. The Wards are acknowledged by other Travellers to be one of the "oldest families on the road." The name itself is the anglicized form of *Mac an Bhaird,* which in Irish means "son of the bard." Bards—like the early smiths—had a long history of itinerancy in Ireland, travelling the countryside telling stories and composing poetry and ballads in exchange for food and lodging. In the seventeenth and eighteenth centuries, they were identified by the British as symbols of native Irish culture and singled out for suppression. Faced with imprisonment for reciting Irish poems and ballads, bards were forced to go underground. Some may have adopted other itinerant trades in order to travel less conspicuously. Like many other native Irish seeking to escape

repression at the hands of the English, they anglicized their name.

12. Approximately 200,000 Irish volunteered and fought for the British in World War I; an estimated 60,000 never returned.

13. January 21, 1919—the day the IRA attacked a British police convoy at Soloheadbeg, County Tipperary—is usually given as the beginning of the "Troubles," Ireland's war of independence against the British and subsequent civil war. It was also the day the new Irish Assemby, Dáil Éireann, met for the first time in Dublin after Sinn Féin's sweeping victory in the elections of the previous year. The fighting that broke out between Irish guerrillas and the British Army and its auxillary forces—the infamous Black and Tans—lasted for two and a half years. A truce was declared in July 1921; the Anglo-Irish Treaty was signed in December and ratified in January the following year by a slim majority of Dáil Éireann. (Not everyone was satisfied with the Dominion status granted the "Free State" and even less so with the partioning of Northern Ireland.) The British army then withdrew, but soon a civil war broke out between pro-Treaty and anti-Treaty Irish forces, finally ending in May 1923.

14. A *vock* is an endearment.

15. It was a hard economic fact that few poor and working-class parents were able to maintain a child at home much past age fourteen, especially if there were many children in the family. Even in England— which was far better off then Ireland in the 1930s—it is estimated that 70 percent of all children began earning money at fourteen and over 90 percent by age fifteen.

16. The term "friend" was also used by Irish country people to refer to relatives.

17. Until the early 20th century, matched marriages were common throughout rural Ireland. Among the settled population, however, an important purpose was to ensure that property and land were transferred between suitable families. Among Travellers there was little real property, and matches were primarily a way of solidifying kinship bonds and social relationships. Frequently intermarried families have a sense of oneness and solidarity expressed in remarks such as "There's no differ between them, they're married in through one another" and "We're all the one."

18. Despite Ireland's neutrality during the war—refered to in Ireland as the "emergency"—it feared a German attack and increased its army to 250,000 men. In addition, 50,000 people from the Republic volunteered to serve in the British army. Throughout the countryside, villagers spelled out the letters E I R E in large painted stones so that overhead bombers would not make a mistake. In April and May 1941

German aircraft had bombed Belfast; nearly 900 people lost their lives, 10,000 became homeless after fires swept the city, and 100,000 fled to the countryside.

19. Northern Ireland's newly established aircraft industry built 1,500 bombers after December 1941. One hundred fifty ships were produced in Belfast's shipyards between 1939–43. The traditional linen industry was expanded into the production of uniforms, tents, and parachutes.

20. The B-Specials were an all-Protestant paramilitary police reserve much feared by Catholics in Northern Ireland. They were replaced in the early 1970s by the nominally nonsectarian Ulster Defense Regiment.

21. Connemara is best known to the outsider for its wild beauty and small, sturdy ponies. It has long been one of the poorest parts of the country. Although comparatively prosperous today, it is still remote and traditional and remains a *Gaeltacht* or Irish-speaking area.

22. Before their large-scale migration to urban areas beginning in the 1960s, most Travellers were localized, seldom venturing beyond two or three counties. (Only the families specializing in horse dealing—known as "blockers"—travelled across country.) As a result, there was a certain territoriality. Faction fights between rival "clans," especially between families from the west and the east, were a feature of country fairs in the early part of this century. Usually the fighting stopped when the blood began to flow. Then the two sides would make up, at least for the moment, and soothe their pains with drink. But long-standing emnities also existed between certain families.

23. In a widely publicized incident in 1968, residents of Rahoon, a housing estate on the outskirts of Galway City, picketed a proposed official campsite in their area and forced the city to abandon work on it. A year later, a group of residents still angry because several Traveller families remained camped near the abandoned site armed themselves with sticks and attacked the families. They uprooted tents and physically pushed the Travellers and their belongings into the street. This incident gave rise to a new word in the national lexicon, "rahoonery," meaning violently anti-Traveller sentiment and action.

24. Travelling women seldom, if ever, ride horses. Only adolescent boys ride with any regularity, and then usually when they are rounding up horses that have wandered away during the night.

25. In 1963, Grattan Puxon, a twenty-five-year-old Englishmen with a Gypsy background, visited Ireland and was moved by the poverty and harassment of Travelling People. He formally organized the Itinerant Action Group and helped them clarify their aims and objectives. The group was determined to see that the recommendations contained in the government's *Report of the Commission on Itinerancy* (1963) to build

a network of sites and make housing and education available to Travellers be implemented. They resisted evictions, picketed government offices, marked through Dublin, and opened their own makeshift primary school on a piece of wasteland in a Dublin suburb. The school was torn down a week later by Corporation workers attempting to evict the families. In February 1964 Gratton Puxon was arrested on a possession of explosives charge—he maintained his innocence—and subsequently returned to England.

26. Nan's brother Joe Donohoe played an early role in working for a better life for Travellers. In December 1960 he led a deputation of Travellers to meet with the Commission on Itinerancy to complain about frequent evictions and request legal places to camp. Together with Gratton Puxon, Joe was one of the main forces behind the short-lived Itinerant Action Group. At most the group had about 150 men, women, and children supporters—including Nan's family—who occupied twenty trailers on the south side of Dublin. Joe Donohoe became chairperson of the Itinerant Action Group in 1964.

27. Today the fields, hedgerows, and large trees bordering Holylands are gone, swallowed up by the expansion of the suburbs. Rows of two-story stucco homes for middle-class families now stand where Travellers once grazed their horses. An enormous shopping mall has been built at the bottom of the laneway leading to the site. Holylands has also been developed. In the mid-1970s the Dublin Corporation built small chalets with indoor plumbing for most of the families on the site. In 1984 these were replaced with more substantial structures—small versions of the homes settled people live in. The Maughams and Donohoes no longer live on the site, only the Connors remain.

FURTHER READING

Gmelch, George. *The Irish Tinkers: The Urbanization of an Itinerant People.* 2d ed. Prospect Heights, Ill.: Waveland Press, 1985.
Examines the cityward migration of Travellers in the 1960s and 1970s and their adjustment to urban life.

Gmelch, George, and Kroup, Ben. *To Shorten the Road.* Dublin: The O'Brien Press and Toronto: Macmillan, 1978.
Folktales collected from Irish Travellers—many from Nan's grandmother and uncle—traditional as well as an introduction to travelling life.

Gmelch, Sharon Bohn. *Tinkers and Travellers.* Photographs by Pat Langan and George Gmelch. Dublin: The O'Brien Press and Montreal: McGill-Queens University Press, 1975.
A general introduction to Traveller culture. Many of the photographs are of the families of Holylands.

MacMahon, Bryan. *The Honey Spike.* Dublin: The Talbot Press, 1972.
An entertaining novel about Travellers.

Maher, Sean. *The Road To God Knows Where.* Dublin: The Talbot Press, 1972.
A Traveller autobiography.

Synge, John Millington. *The Tinker's Wedding: A Comedy in Two Acts.* Dublin: Maunsel and Co., 1907.
J. M. Synge's classic play about Travelling People.

Travelling Review Body. *Report of the Travelling People Review Body.* Dublin: The Stationery Office, 1983.
The most recent government report on Travelling People, providing information on numbers, settlement, education, and health.

Wiedel, Janine and Martina O'Fearadhaigh. *Irish Tinkers.* London: Lattimer, 1976.
A photographic essay.